DELIVERANCE

To order additional copies of *Deliverance,* by Alla Czerkasij,
call **1-800-765-6955**.
Visit us at **www.reviewandherald.com**
for information on other Review and Herald® products.

DELIVERANCE

ALLA CZERKASIJ WITH
NATALIE CZERKASIJ LEWELLEN

REVIEW AND HERALD® PUBLISHING ASSOCIATION
Since 1861 | www.reviewandherald.com

Published by Review and Herald® Publishing Association, Hagerstown, MD 21741-1119

Review and Herald® titles may be purchased in bulk for educational, business, fund-raising, or sales promotional use. For information, e-mail SpecialMarkets@reviewandherald.com.

The Review and Herald® Publishing Association publishes biblically based materials for spiritual, physical, and mental growth and Christian discipleship.

The author assumes full responsibility for the accuracy of all facts and quotations as cited in this book.

Scripture quotations marked NLT are taken from the *Holy Bible,* New Living Translation, copyright © 1996, 2004, 2007 by Tyndale House Foundation. Used by permission of Tyndale House Publishers, Inc., Carol Stream, Illinois 60188. All rights reserved.

This book was
Edited by JoAlyce Waugh
Copyedited by Delma Miller
Designed by Daniel Añez/Review and Herald® Design Center
Cover art by Robert Hunt
Typeset: Minion Pro 11/13

PRINTED IN U.S.A.

18 17 16 15 14   5 4 3 2 1

Library of Congress Cataloging-in-Publication Data
Czerkasij, Alla.
  Deliverance / Alla Czerkasij ; with Natalie Lewellen.
    pages cm
  ISBN 978-0-8280-2715-1
1. Czerkasij, Alla. 2. Seventh-Day Adventist converts--Biography. 3.
World War, 1939-1945--Biography. I. Title.
  BX6193.C94A3 2014
  286.7092--dc23
  [B]
                            2012049331

[12-9-12 App made]

ISBN 978-0-8280-2715-1

DEDICATION

For Father Nikolai,
who died so young and tragically,
and
Mother Eudokia,
for her unfailing courage and love for life,
and
all the innocents who suffered during World War II.

ACKNOWLEDGMENTS

First and foremost, I wish to thank my longtime friend, Elly Edson, for coming up with the idea of writing a book in the first place. That was 35 years ago, and she hasn't quit "hounding" me since!

A heartfelt thank-you to the many teachers for their faith in me, and who allowed me to share my story with their students over the years. (You know who you are!) And to all the precious students who listened with such rapt attention—you were my greatest encouragers and supporters, writing me numerous letters with the plea "Write a book!" I treasure each and every one of you. And to the many people in other audiences who always welcomed me with such graciousness and kindness. I always felt at home with you.

A special thank-you to Anne R. Clark for her meticulous and impeccable work; and for never giving up on me through this long process.

I extend my deep appreciation to Jack J. Blanco, Ralph Neall, and Beatrice Neall for their time, interest, and valuable advice; even more, for their precious friendships.

I am so very grateful and blessed for the love and support of my entire family, especially my husband, Wesley, and my son-in-law, Jim, for the countless hours they so generously and patiently gave, while my daughter, Natalie, and I hammered away at this project. It was a long process with difficult interruptions, but with Natalie by my side on this roller-coaster ride, I wouldn't have wanted to be anywhere else. I love you, dear daughter.

There are no words to describe my gratitude to all the soldiers in the Allied Forces who fought so bravely and gave of themselves so freely—many with their very lives—for me, and for you, dear reader, so that we may live and enjoy the gift of freedom.

Above all, I praise and thank my God for His gift of life and love, and for the wondrous ways He has carried me through this life.

INTRODUCTION

While there are many concentration/labor camp stories from World War II, *Deliverance* is unique. In this story the Ukrainian family was oppressed by Communists under Stalin then by the invading German army, and transported to Germany to work in labor camps. It climaxes with their deliverance by the American military and, finally, breathing the fresh air of liberty in the United States.

Alla's survival is nothing but miraculous. As a young girl she experiences the horrors of that era yet lives to tell her story. However, her story does not end with her "deliverance," but continues with one divine providential leading after another. From Germany to Sweden, then to America, where she meets her husband, who is also from the Ukraine and had been in the same displaced persons camp at Augsburg.

Without a doubt, God has been watching over the little girl from the Ukraine and has kept drawing her closer and closer to Himself, leading her step by step to the truth as found in Scripture. Having given her heart to Jesus Christ and being totally in love with her Savior, she has no hesitation in lifting Him up at every opportunity. She has been telling others about her "deliverance," not only from the hardships of war but also of her spiritual deliverance. Readers of her story will be blessed and will find courage to face the difficulties of life just as she did.

Even though Alla and I did not meet until recently, we were both prisoners in Leipzig, Germany, labor camps during the war. It is with the utmost sincerity that I recommend this book.

—Jack J. Blanco
Professor Emeritus
Southern Adventist University

Chapter 1

Leipzig, Germany
Spring, 1944

Wake up, Alla! Let's run!" Mother's voice was soft but urgent, and I could feel her gently shaking me.

The warning sirens were howling in the night, and thunderous explosions surrounded our home of two years—a flimsy, gray, single-story barracks with small, dirty windows. We lived in a labor camp surrounded by armed guards, German shepherds, and barbed-wire fencing. Once again the Allies were nearing the city of Leipzig, Germany.

Detecting the seriousness in Mother's voice, and fully dressed as always, I got up and held her hand as we raced across the bare concrete floor to the door of our tiny room. Nearing the door, Mother turned back to wake Tina, our roommate, whose husband was in Buchenwald concentration camp along with my father. She slept on the lower bunk bed with her arms wrapped around her 5-year-old daughter. We could see them plainly during the intermittent flashes of exploding bombs. Mother, in her mid-20s and a little older than Tina, felt responsible for their safety.

"Come on, Tina. Wake up! Let's run!" coaxed my mother. "Don't you hear the planes nearing?" But Mother's pleas fell on deaf ears.

"Oh, just leave me alone!" replied Tina, sounding tired and annoyed. "I don't care anymore whether I live or die. You go ahead and run."

We all were exhausted from the nightly routine of evacuating the barracks several times, but only a few precious minutes might separate life from death, and we didn't have time to argue. The droning of the planes was growing louder as they approached the camp.

We rushed from our corner room, and I ran as fast as my little legs could carry me toward the entrance of our bomb shelter in an underground bunker. Just before we reached the shelter, we heard a tremendous explosion and instinctively turned our heads to see where the bomb had landed. It had hit our room directly where Tina and her daughter slept. As flames from the explosion lit the sky, Mother and I looked at one another wordlessly. At that moment we both realized that there must have been a reason we were spared and that God must have a purpose for our lives.

Eastern Ukraine
Years before World War II

My father, Nikolai, was a gentle, fun-loving, idealistic young man who enjoyed writing poems. He had a fair complexion, brown hair, blue eyes, and a slight build. He suffered from rheumatic fever, was the second of four brothers, and had a younger sister, Katya. His father, my grandpa Anton, was a carpenter, and his mother, my babushka Natasha, was a homemaker. By the age of 26 she had given birth to five children. They were poor, and Grandpa Anton's parents lived with them. Yet they had a cow, a vegetable garden, and an orchard. Babushka Natasha was well respected in her village, which was located in the coal-mining region of Donbas in eastern Ukraine. She was a hardworking woman who kept her home tidy and her children clean, and had lots of common sense. She couldn't read or write, but was practical, dignified, and not a gossip. Grandpa Anton adored her and made their home comfortable by crafting furniture and cabinets. He was also known to often help neighbors with repairs at no charge.

Because both of them believed strongly in education and wanted a better life for their children, they sent Nikolai 43.5 miles (70 kilometers) away from home to study engineering at a trade school located near the city of Slavyansk.

One day Nikolai decided to take a look at the roster of new arrivals posted on the bulletin board and noticed another last name like his own: Szczerbak. He thought it might be some distant relative and decided to investigate.

He and his roommate, Alex, went to the girls' dormitory to look up that girl, Dusia (short for Eudokia) Szczerbak, and get things straightened out. Greeted at the door by a pretty, petite girl with large brown eyes, the boys stated their request to see the new girl, Dusia. The adorable girl with the ready smile informed them that she was the one they were seeking. Her roommate, Lydia, was with her, and the four students talked for a while, discovering in the process that Nikolai and Dusia were not related. As Nikolai turned to leave, he said to Dusia, "One day, doll, you are going to be mine." He was 17 years old; she was 14.

My cheerful, energetic mother, Dusia, grew up on a farm near the tiny village of Hruchseva, which was in a rural area near the city of Slavyansk. Her father, my grandpa Gregory, had been a widower when he married my grandma Barbara. Barbara's parents died when typhoid fever swept through Russia and the Ukraine, leaving her and her two older sisters orphans. Life was hard, so the sisters arranged for Barbara to marry a certain young man when she was 17. Her new in-laws decided to move to Siberia in search of a better life. Siberia is a large place with areas that have woods full of edible mushrooms, oak trees for building cottages and log homes, and rivers brimming with fresh water and fish. It is not all snow and ice. But because the marriage was one of convenience and not love, and Siberia was so far away, Barbara ran away.

She landed a job as a housekeeper on Grandpa Gregory's farm. His wife had been stricken with typhoid fever and lay in bed, dying. There were three children: a 13-year-old daughter, an 11-year-old son, and a 3-year-old boy, Peter. The dying mother noticed Barbara's love for and devotion to the children, and before she died she begged Barbara not to leave them. Barbara promised she wouldn't and stayed.

About six months after the funeral, Grandpa Gregory and Barbara were riding in a horse-drawn cart to deliver produce to the city. He put his arm around her shoulder and said, "Well, Barb, why don't we just get married?" He was 36 and she was 18. The deal was struck, and life went on, with much work to do on the farm.

The children loved Barbara, a hardworking young woman with a tremendous sense of humor. But the marriage was not a happy one. Grandpa Gregory had a drinking problem and abused her. When the boys grew up, they stood up for her, but when they left home, she had no one to defend her. Yet her husband was known to be generous in his village; he invented primitive but helpful harvesting machinery, helped the less fortunate, and supported education. He signed his name with an X not because he lacked intelligence, but because he was never given the opportunity to go to school.

My mother was born to this union. They also had a son who died of mumps in infancy, and later came Alexa, the joy of Barbara's life. Barbara was a deeply religious woman who attended the Greek Orthodox Church faithfully and sang in the choir with Dusia by her side. As a little girl, Dusia saw a picture depicting John the Baptist's head on a charger and was so frightened that she hid her face in her mother's skirt. All through her life her religious experience was dampened because of that gory sight.

One early summer day Grandpa Gregory stood in his wheat field of many acres, checking the crop's progress, when suddenly a most beautiful woman dressed in full traditional Ukrainian garb appeared before him. Her face sad, she spoke to him: "Ukraine is going to suffer much." And then she vanished. There were no trees, bushes, or rocks in the field that she could have gone behind, and Grandpa Gregory was stunned. The apparition and her words left him puzzled, but he would soon understand.

In 1932 the Soviet leadership created a tremendous artificial famine in the Ukraine. The Ukrainian peasants were forced to submit to Communism. Their farms and lands were confiscated, and collectivism was initiated fully. During this short and brutal time approximately 7 million Ukrainians were starved to death, their fields burned, and the grain carted off to Russia. Anyone trying to hide food or take so much as a handful of grain was either shot or sent to Siberia. Cannibalism was known to have occurred because of this famine.

During that time my mother was about 16 years old and was a member of a Communist youth group called Pioneers. They wore uniforms with red scarves and were indoctrinated in atheism and other Communistic ideology. Taken from the classroom every so often, they were armed with pitchforks and sent into the fields to collect and bury the piles of corpses in mass graves. My mother had heard that relief had been sent from America under the Hoover Relief Plan to aid the starving population, but the world didn't know that it was our own government that orchestrated the famine or that all the people were given was toothpaste and toothbrushes.

Nikolai and Dusia were dating by this time, as were their roommates, Alex and Lydia. Nikolai knew his family was literally starving, and because the students were given ration cards, he was able to obtain some bread, flour, and potatoes. Dusia gave him her own rations as well, and he climbed on top of a train car and rode home. There he made soup and stayed to feed his family until their strength and sanity returned. Meanwhile, Dusia sneaked into the local fields, risking arrest, and gleaned corn to keep herself alive.

Later, when my parents married, his family had a great love for their daughter-in-law because she had sacrificed to help save their lives.

Dusia fell deeply in love with Nikolai, and he adored her. One day while walking through the deserted streets in the village, he looked at his beautiful bride-to-be, picked her up, and carried her in his arms. As they were nearing an intersection, his uncle happened to come around the corner. Nikolai was so surprised and embarrassed to be caught in such a display of affection considered unmanly in our culture that he dropped her onto the ground and let her lie at his feet!

But their love was pure and full of dreams. In 1934, after Dusia received a degree in chemistry, they were married in a very simple ceremony, and each was accepted by the other's family.

The engineering program had been eliminated before Nikolai was able to complete his degree, so he ended up working in a factory. Dusia worked briefly as a laboratory technician at the same factory, but shortly thereafter was assigned by the Soviet government to work on a collective farm. Having grown up on a farm, she was familiar with the work involved and was appointed a forewoman.

was born on December 6, 1935. Mother was only 18 years old, and Father was almost 22. Mother's labor pains were horrific, and she spent many hours in excruciating pain. With no relief to be had, she lay writhing on bedding placed on the dirt floor of a makeshift hospital, which was really just a shack. Mother was alone except for a so-called midwife, who sat on a chair in a corner, not knowing what to do. A pair of male workers was in the ceiling above installing an electric cable. By the time I was born, she explained to me later, she felt no love for me. During the course of my life she often reminded me of the pain she had suffered because of me, for which I always apologized and felt guilty.

Father, however, was playful and tenderhearted. I remember once when he came home from work with a half-eaten sandwich and said, "As I was walking through the field, a rabbit came running toward me. He had this bread in his mouth and wanted it delivered to Alla, a nice little girl he had heard about." I ate it with great gusto.

Mother was a practical person with an independent spirit. She told me years later that she had no patience for Father's "idealistic nonsense," but I loved him all the more for his gentleness. Mother administered corporal punishment often, which was usually well deserved. Being the only grandchild, however, I was also adored by doting grandparents, uncles, and Aunt Katya, my father's younger sister.

When I was a newborn, it was important to my parents that I be baptized. Infant mortality was high, mostly because of a lack of sanitary conditions. Since we had no baby food, young mothers would chew food, spit it onto a teaspoon, and feed it to the baby. Or when the baby was sleepy, it would be given a homemade pacifier: chewed-up food from the mother's mouth placed on a small square of cheesecloth and tied up with a thread, which formed a small ball for the baby to suck on. Sometimes this pacifier would fall out of the baby's mouth and in no time be covered with flies. We had no screens, and during hot weather the windows were wide open. The mother would simply wave away the flies and put the pacifier back into the child's mouth. The flies bred fast since we were surrounded by animals and outhouses, and disease was common since no medicines or antibiotics were available.

Therefore, it was imperative for parents to have their babies christened by the age of 6 or 7 weeks. Otherwise, according to the folklore of a culture heavily steeped in superstition cloaked in the garb of religion, their souls would be destined to ages of limbo. Such babies were not allowed to be buried in cemeteries, so their graves were dug outside the walls.

Even in our literature and poetry written by famous authors, you find stories of those little outcasts swinging on the branches of willow trees that grew on the shores of the river. It was believed that you could see them only at midnight if there was a full moon. This frightened even the most stalwart, and no one ventured out that late. However, if they did go out that late, they still held to this belief, although nothing was seen.

Now, my young parents cared a great deal about me and didn't want me to end up dangling on a willow branch like a little monkey throughout eternity. Baptisms, however, were not permitted, since religion had been outlawed in our country. So at great risk to their freedom and their lives, they convinced a former priest, along with a set of godparents, to baptize me secretly in the middle of the night. Later when Mother told me how those five people dedicated me to God with fear and trembling, it touched my heart. Such love, such courage!

My parents also had to give gifts to the priest and godparents, such as sausages, potatoes, flour, and eggs—no money, just something life-sustaining.

Through the years, though, I found myself unable to accept a theology that painted such a negative picture about God's character. How much easier it is to accept and believe what is written in the Bible, that the dead know nothing (see Eccl. 9:5). They are not swinging on branches, but sleeping in their graves until Jesus comes and takes them home to heaven to be there with Him forever.

Another story Mother related to me with regard to our superstitions involved a trip we took to the village where her half sister lived. It was deep in the countryside where secret customs and beliefs prevailed. As we settled ourselves in the train, we sat across from a beautiful Gypsy girl. I was just a toddler and smiled happily, as did the passenger across from us. To my great delight, she ended up holding me and playing with me. But as it came time for us to disembark, I began crying and refused to part with my newfound friend. By the time we got to my aunt's house, I was inconsolable. I wouldn't stop crying. Mother told her half sister about my attraction to the Gypsy, and they decided that she must have cast a spell on me.

Almost every village had a *Baba Schepotukh*a (Grandma the Whisperer), so they took me to her. She brewed some herbs while whispering incantations, then gave me a drink of her concoction, and I fell soundly asleep. I am sure I cried because I hadn't had a nap, and *Baba Schepotukha* made tea that knocked me out. She also had to be paid in goods.

Those babas were feared and revered, for they could also cast bad spells and, thus, had a powerful influence over the villagers. If a girl was in love with a young man and he wasn't interested, she would just go see a baba. Some brew would be made, the young woman had to give it to her heartthrob to drink, and he would fall madly in love with her.

Many of these beliefs originated from heathenism and played a large part in our culture when I was a child.

Babushka Natasha, my father's mother, had an aunt we called Baba Maryna. She was a toothless woman in her 70s, her complexion was leathery and wrinkled from constant exposure to the sun and cold weather, and she was considered ancient. Although she was small in stature, she was strong from years of hard physical labor. Her hair tightly pulled back into a bun, she wore a large white apron that reached almost to her ankles. With it she wiped her hands and sweaty face and blew her nose, and when I came by with my face smudged with dirt, that apron came in handy. We had no wipes.

In the summer evenings when the air began to cool and the supper dishes were put away, I remember Baba Maryna and the other elderly women of the village sitting on their doorsteps, catching up on gossip. They gummed roasted sunflower and pumpkin seeds and spit out the shells, which mostly collected on their chins and weren't wiped off. They just let the shells slide down onto their aprons.

In her younger days, she and her husband had owned a mill, which used to stand by our river Torets. Covered with green algae and protruding from the river, the supports of the mill were all that was left—a reminder of the past. Once during laundry time, Mother pointed to those mill poles and said, "You know, *Allachka* [little Alla], those poles saved your life when you were 8 months old. One day I came to do the laundry and put you next to me in an enamel basin. As I bent down to pick up the clothes to wash, I looked up and you were gone. I could see the empty basin floating down the river. Then I spotted you. The wavelets were tossing you up against the mill poles, which were keeping your head above water. I threw myself into the water and grabbed you. Water poured out of your nose and mouth, and I shook you in desperation and fear. Then you cried, and I knew you would be all right."

Baba Maryna also owned a plot of land, but lived in a dilapidated house. She was a widow with no children, and since she was getting old, a family council meeting was held, presided over by Babushka Natasha. Since my parents had nothing, it was decided that a new house would be built on the property for us to live in, with an extra room for Baba Maryna so that my parents could take care of her until her dying day.

When the day came to begin the project, Grandpa Gregory, my mother's father, who was big, strong, and no stranger to hard work, arrived. Along with him came Grandpa Anton, my father's father, with his carpentry skills. The old shack was torn down, and we began to dig the foundation. It was a village affair—the men mixed clay and straw for the foundation before fashioning a brick oven in the yard for the women to cook lunch in. Half the women formed a circle, putting their arms around one another, and started dancing and singing while stirring the clay mixture with their feet. The rest of the women baked bread, cooked potatoes, picked fresh fruits from the trees, and sang also while they prepared lunch. Even the occasion of building our house was turned into a grand celebration by the villagers.

Meanwhile Father cut reeds from the river, lined them up in our front yard, and let them dry in the sun for the thatched roof. But standing in the cold water day after day made him ill, and later he developed rheumatic fever—at least that's what Mother believed. One side effect of his illness was that he was not drafted into the Soviet Army before the Germans invaded the Ukraine—his general health was poor and he was believed to have a heart condition.

At the end of the day we all went to the river Torets to wash up before bedtime. Even then the men continued working, catching fish with a net so we could have even more food to eat and share the next day.

Since we had no washcloths, our mothers would break up sunflower heads into chunks, dip them into the water, and scrub our tender skin. It was painful, but we were clean; and with our blood circulating well, we slept soundly.

By late fall our house was finished, and all four of us moved in. It was modern by our standards—we had electricity! Mother still carried water, however, from a well quite distant from our house, and we continued to use an outhouse. Laundry and bathing during the summer would continue to be done in the river. On our dirt floor we spread fresh grass, which smelled so good. For heating, cooking, and baking, we used a wood-burning stove. We had it made and were happy.

While Mother and Father were away at work, Baba Maryna was my babysitter. Since she never had a child of her own, I became hers. I remember she had a hope chest that contained linens, pillowcases, and towels in which she hid apples between the folds. She would reward me with one for good behavior—but this behavior never lasted long. I loved getting into trouble and was always fighting with the neighborhood children, even if I was the one getting beat up.

When we first began living together, we all got along well. Then Baba Maryna discovered Mother was not a "smart woman." The proof was in a barrel of pickled tomatoes.

It was harvesttime, both on the collective farm and at home. We built a large underground root cellar across the yard from our house. Father dug holes in the cellar walls, hauled sand from the riverbank, and filled the cavities with it. In the sand we buried beets, carrots, and turnips. Potatoes we dried in the sun a bit to keep them from rotting, and then stored them in wooden bins in the root cellar. We also packed barrels of pickled cucumbers, tomatoes, and sauerkraut mixed with shredded carrots and whole apples.

When it came time to pickle the tomatoes, however, Baba Maryna instructed Mother on how much salt to use. But her advice fell on deaf ears. Mother felt that because she had a degree in chemistry, she could calculate on her own how much salt was required per barrel, and didn't need instructions. The result was disastrous. The tomatoes were much too salty to eat, and a whole barrel of them was almost completely wasted. Baba Maryna picked out the oversalted tomatoes, one by one, and took them around the village, encouraging neighbors to taste and see what a poor choice my father had made by marrying my mother.

Of course Mother's reputation was ruined among the older citizens. However, that only lasted until the Germans occupied our village and took many of our young boys and girls, including my aunt Katya, Father's younger sister, to work in factories in Germany. Then all those older village women whose children and grandchildren had been taken away came to Mother for help. The villagers, most of them illiterate, needed someone to write letters to their loved ones, and Mother did it for them. The letters always began: "Greetings from home, from our village, and from our little chickens and our little goats. They bow to you. We all miss you." Mother had a hard time suppressing her smiles. She was a good sport, and held no grudges. In fact, both she and Father laughed about the whole tomato matter. But not Babushka Natasha. She felt her aunt Maryna's gossip was dishonorable and breached family loyalty. Ultimately, Mother's reputation was restored among the villagers, and the tomato fiasco forgiven and forgotten.

By this time Communism was in full swing. Life was very oppressive, and we began to live in constant fear. Neighbors reported on one another to the authorities and would be arrested, beaten, and jailed for the least of offenses or even because of grudges. Teachers would ask students if their parents prayed at home, which caused parents to fear that their children might be taken away.

When Father worked at the factory, he was ordered by his supervisor to report on a certain coworker, stating when and where they met and the content of their conversations. A week later he was asked into the office to report his meetings. He did not want to squeal on the man, so he was not truthful. Instead he claimed they did not meet nor talk, not realizing that the coworker had been ordered to spy on him as well and had reported their meetings. As punishment for Father's lack of cooperation, the supervisor removed his gun from his holster and pistol-whipped Father in the head.

One morning Father happened to oversleep. He panicked, knowing what would happen when he arrived late for work: he would be accused of undermining the country and its regime, considered an enemy of the state, and charged with treason.

It was March, and the ground was still frozen. Terrified, Father repeatedly threw himself onto his knees, trying to injure himself and fake an accident. Mother ran to get the village doctor, who had little medical training. He came and examined Father's heart, which was beating wildly. As he lay there in bed, two KGB men rode into our yard on horseback. They saw the doctor, who explained to them Father had had a heart attack. "Get well soon, *Towarischt* [Comrade] Szczerbak," they sneered. "Our country needs workers."

The tall, well-built officer with shiny, black boots turned to me and smirked, "Your father is going to die."

"No!" I cried defiantly. "He will not die." I was 6 years old and loved my father dearly, but I was scared.

Father would later be transferred to the local railroad station. His job was to direct trains, and one day he came home pale and shaken. A train with windowless boxcars had stopped at the station, and he could hear screams and banging from inside the cars. People were crying and begging for help. He could only guess their final destination.

I was finally old enough to start attending school, and oh, how I loved it. One day when I came home after classes, I yearned for a nice, juicy, sweet onion. We had rows and rows of them in our garden, but so did our neighbor next door. I decided to pull up one of his. The neighbor appeared out of nowhere. "And what do you think you are doing stealing my onions?" he demanded.

Caught red-handed, I had no answer. He took my ear and twisted it hard and then did the same to the other. It was painful, but the humiliation was worse. Just then Mother arrived, and seeing me standing there with my ears red like beets and an onion full of dirt hanging from my hand, she immediately understood the situation. Very calmly she lifted my dress from behind (for better impact) and gave me a sound spanking. I decided then and there that the onion had not been worth all the pain and humiliation I experienced that day, and my tendency for theft was instantly cured.

Chapter **6**

My education and happiness were short-lived. Both ended six months later when the German and Soviet armies first appeared and took turns occupying our village. Besides feeding them, we were constantly under fire because our village was located directly on the front, and we were caught in the crossfire between the two armies.

My first encounter with the Germans was the day I watched three soldiers drive into our front yard in a horse-drawn wagon. They strode into my mother's kitchen and started eating her borscht, a cabbage-and-beet soup, straight out of the pot. They were unshaven, dirty, and covered with dust.

Their next move was to search the house for more food or anything of value they could carry off, which wasn't much, since we were poor villagers. Then I saw them carry a chest from our shed. *That was too much!* I thought. They could have Mother's borscht, which could be replaced, but not the chest. It contained the precious pig we had recently slaughtered and processed. Now they were placing it on the wagon. It was our sustenance for the winter months, and they were taking it away, not to mention that the pig had meant a lot to me.

Mother, who was still working as a forewoman on a collective farm, had been encouraged to compete with the other forewomen. The forewoman of the group that planted and seeded the fastest and harvested the most would receive a nice prize. Mother's prize for winning was a piglet that became my pet and my love.

That fall, as winter was nearing and the weather became colder, our piglet was transferred from the shed to the house, much to my delight. It had blue eyes, white eyelashes, and a round pink snout. It slept next to my bed and made little oinking noises, and it became my close companion.

The following summer Mother continued feeding it corn, potatoes mixed with chaff, beets, and pumpkins, and it grew by leaps and bounds. Then one day I heard a horrible squealing. Father was killing the pig! I was horrified and covered my ears as I ran from the yard, heartbroken.

24

The next day Babushka Natasha came to help Mother and Baba Maryna make sausages, slice bacon strips, and cut chunks of ham. The fat was saved for frying potatoes. I was sad, but young as I was, I knew it was food necessary for our survival.

And now the Germans had the nerve to cart it off!

At that moment my parents were at the other end of the village at the miller's place, grinding our wheat into flour. I ran as fast as I could to tell them the terrible news. I was confident Father would scare off those soldiers and retrieve our pig.

My parents hurried home. "Comrades," my father pleaded earnestly, "please do not take our pig away." He knew some German because he and Mother had been taught the language in school.

One of the soldiers pointed a gun at my father's chest. "Choose between your life and the pig," he said gruffly.

Unarmed and outnumbered, Father chose life. But I was disappointed; in my immaturity I had really thought he would scare them off.

Before Communism had really begun to weigh us down, the people in our village had lived fairly harmonious lives. Depending on where the Soviets needed us, adults either worked in factories or on collective farms where they planted and harvested. On weekends they tended their own gardens, chickens, pigs, cows, and goats. Except for the occasional gossip or disagreements, neighbors got along well and lived by an unwritten code: we looked out for one another in every way possible and tried to make life easier for all.

But the longer the Germans occupied our village, the more we villagers became afraid and suspicious of one another. Trust fled, and it seemed as though everyone was our enemy, even in our own homes. Some wives began flirting brazenly with German soldiers, and the husbands feared the soldiers would beat them if they reprimanded their wives or attempted to restrain them.

Mother's ability to speak German fairly well came in handy now. One day two neighboring families got into an argument. To solve the problem, one family, who really felt offended, went to the German officers stationed in our village and accused their neighbors of being collaborators with the Soviets. The whole village went into an uproar because everyone knew it was not true. Mother, a good communicator, spoke up in defense of the accused neighbors. Thankfully, the case was dropped because there was no evidence, and to everyone's relief, life continued as usual.

When the Germans occupied our village, they also made themselves comfortable in our homes and slept in our beds, leaving us to sleep on the floor. We watched them get up early in the morning to shave, wash, and exercise. They groomed their horses and polished their boots to a shine.

One day Mother carried two heavy pails of water on a yoke from the well quite a distance away. A German soldier took the water from her and gave it to his horses. He did this again on her second trip from the well. On the third trip, Mother lost her temper and cursed him in German. He was so shocked and infuriated that he pointed his rifle at her and yelled, "I'll shoot you, you Russian swine!" Mother curled up into a fetal position and waited to die. After that, she was required to carry water for the horses on a daily basis, and she did not protest anymore.

Many girls and young women hid in root cellars, sheds, and barns in the evenings because they did not want to make themselves available to the soldiers. But not all did so. Some, including married women, liked the soldiers. However, during the times when the Soviets temporarily regained control of our village, the husbands would no longer fear their unfaithful wives, and some of those women sported bruised and battered faces. These women lost the respect of their families and the villagers.

The Germans occupied our village for several months. The first waves of their forces were brutal, but the divisions that came later were less aggressive toward us. They allowed us the freedom to visit the city of Slavyansk and even to attend the same movie theaters they did. We walked through city streets and parks filled with colorful flower beds and rosebushes. Soldiers, smartly dressed in their uniforms, strolled by with our girls hanging on their arms.

One day Mother took me for a leisurely walk through the park with a friend of hers, a young woman who lived in the city. This friend was better dressed and more educated than we villagers were. Tall and slender, with auburn hair obviously styled by a beautician, this classy woman in her early 20s turned many a soldier's head. She worked as a translator for the Germans, so one thing Mother and she had in common was they both spoke German. Not long after the Germans retreated and we were again occupied by the Soviet Army, Mother's friend was arrested and tried as a spy for the enemy. She was tied to a tree and shot to death. We were horrified. She was just a translator, and now Mother was being called in to give an account of her own "activities" with the Germans.

Apparently, because Mother had previously helped settle the argument between the two feuding neighbors, the accusing family decided to report her as a German sympathizer. Some of our villagers came to Mother's defense and explained to the Soviet authorities that the accusing neighbors had made up the whole story about their innocent neighbors and now they were trying to take revenge on my mother for her interference. The results didn't go well for the accusers. They were yelled at and told that they would be severely punished if they caused any more trouble.

By this time the collective farm had stopped functioning because of the constant fighting between the Germans and the Soviets, so the villagers divided it into plots amongst themselves. The work continued on the fields and in the gardens, not to mention the tending of the animals, and we children had our share of responsibilities as well. We gathered kindling and stacked the wood chopped by our parents, swept the yard, took care of younger siblings, and chased the geese and chickens away from the gardens where they scratched for worms. We climbed the trees and picked fruit for drying, herded the cows to pasture and then back home again in the evenings, hoed the gardens, plucked the feathers from slaughtered geese for blankets, milked the cows, and knitted winter wear—the boys as well as the girls. Even the small children did their share, sitting for hours at a time sorting rocks from dried beans and peas and picking berries and mushrooms in the forests under adult supervision. We searched for eggs that the hens hid in the bushes and grass, gathering them before they could hatch. But sometimes the eggs and hens were so well hidden that they weren't found until a hen appeared on her own, a brood of chicks following close behind.

Babushka Natasha lived about a mile from us. She was a tall, stern-looking woman, but I always sensed the love and tenderness in her. I remember summer evenings as the villagers returned home from their work in the fields. Tired and hungry, they would wash up and have a hearty supper consisting mostly of borscht. For dessert we had cooked millet with mashed pumpkins, which were naturally sweet. On occasion we children would receive a slice of whole-grain bread dipped first in water and then in sugar made from yellow beets. What a treat!

Since our soil was so rich and soft and the climate was warm, we enjoyed the tastiest fruits and vegetables, not to mention all the good nutrients. Sometimes people ask me how I feel about being a vegetarian. Well, I mostly grew up one. We had very little meat; it was a luxury we could not afford.

As the sun set and the evenings grew cool and comfortable after the day's heat, the villagers gathered for singing—and what wonderful singers they were! Mother had a guitar and played pretty well; she was self-taught. When she was 6 years old, Grandpa Gregory had given a neighbor a small calf in exchange for that guitar.

They began by singing the mournful tunes, every song telling a sad love story that had a tragic ending. But soon their spirits would pick up and the village would echo with happy voices. Father sang out of tune, but it did not deter him; he just kept right on.

One such evening as Mother strummed away, Babushka Natasha sat on the grass with me on her lap. I can still feel her strong, loving arms wrapped around my little body. The crickets were chirping in the grass, and I could smell the sweet aroma of flowers. The sky was black, the stars twinkling overhead. Since we had neither cars nor pollution, the sky seemed close, as if I could reach out my hand and touch those glittering stars. And then I heard Babushka Natasha whisper in my ear, "You see those stars? You are as beautiful and precious to me as one of them."

I knew exactly what she meant. When she or other grown-ups spoke about beauty, it always referred to character, demeanor, or behavior. Making reference to a child's physical beauty was considered flattery and was not done. We were kept humble.

That evening would become one of my few and treasured memories of Babushka Natasha.

It was Babushka Natasha who gave me my first instruction in religion as we entered the small, white, simple Greek Orthodox church located not far from our village. "This is God's house," she explained. When the Germans first arrived in our village, we were allowed to restore our churches and worship again, something for which we had been persecuted under the Stalinist regime.

I could smell the incense and beeswax candles and hear a choir singing in harmonious, solemn tones from the rear balcony. Women and children stood on the left side of the church and men on the right, their hats in their hands, all bowing and crossing themselves as the priest waved his censer toward the congregation.

I watched the old bearded priest officiating at the altar and chanting in a deep singsong voice. He wore a golden vestment and on his gray head, a gold miter, studded with precious gems.

Babushka Natasha purchased two candles to place in front of an icon, this one an image of Jesus painted on a gold-plated background and encased in a wooden boxed frame with a glass cover. Ukrainians consider these icons holy and revere them. As my turn came to place a burning candle in the holder, the flame flickered, and in my imagination the picture of Jesus came to life, and He seemed to sternly shake His head at me the way the adults did when we kids misbehaved. I became frightened and felt convicted of my wickedness. Until then, the only time the grown-ups spoke to us about God was when we were being naughty. They would point upward and say, "God will punish you!" Their words created more fear than love.

But what impressed me the most was the solemnity and reverence the grown-ups displayed by their demeanor, and it made a deep and lasting impression on my young mind. I grasped a little of God's importance and majesty, and I felt as if I were on holy ground, which made me want to return to this church. My little heart was touched, and though I couldn't see Him, I longed to know more about this mysterious God. I was about 6 years old at the time, but it was such a memorable experience that I would later continue to attend church services by myself.

other's much younger sister, Alexa, who had developed tuberculosis by this time, and Grandma Barbara came to visit us. Alexa was 14, and I was 7. By this time Grandpa Gregory had died, a broken and disillusioned man. He had been in favor of the new Communist regime in his younger years. The slogan at that time was "Factory for workers and land for farmers." It sounded so just and good and fair, so he had joined the revolution.

He and his sons had been very hard workers and as a result were rich in land, cattle, and grain. However, having accumulated this wealth, he was now considered an "enemy of the people" and had to be treated as such. A successful farmer was considered a "parasite, miser, and greedy," so his prosperous farm was taken away to be turned into a collective farm and his wealth redistributed to the less prosperous. To add insult to injury, the "less prosperous" included men like Billy, the village bum. While the villagers worked, Billy would sit under a tree and chew a blade of grass. As Grandpa Gregory passed by on his horse-drawn wagon, carting bales of hay for his cattle, he would see Billy and say, "Billy, why don't you go out and do some work?"

"Oh, Uncle Gregory, I plan to go fishing," Billy would reply as he continued to gaze at the sky. But that question stung Billy's pride, and Grandpa Gregory would later pay for it.

When the Communists gained power, Billy joined the Communist Party. He was given a uniform and a gun and was put in charge of the village. He formed a young posse and began intimidating and arresting our farmers as their farms were taken away. He took great pleasure in harassing Grandpa Gregory and treating him with contempt, never letting him forget who the boss was now.

Alexa had been taken to a Soviet military hospital, where they operated on her chest and removed the affected area of her lung. The surgery was done without anesthesia or pain medicine. They closed her wound and placed her in a hammock so they could rock her gently in an effort to lessen the pain. The nurses, doctors, and even hardened soldiers, were loving and tenderhearted toward her. They also had to shave her head. Our sanitary conditions were very poor on the whole, and this was the most effective treatment for lice.

Finally the day came when she was released and could go home. Grandma Barbara decided to bring her to our house where they would find the comfort of a loving family and moral support, which they did—with the exception of one spoiled, selfish person.

I resented all the attention Alexa was receiving, and my jealousy knew no bounds. One day I spotted her sitting on a tree stump in the middle of our yard enjoying much-needed sunshine and fresh air. There she sat with her bald head. Her mother, standing on the front steps of the house, looked at her ever so lovingly and said to my mother, "Look at her, Dusia. Doesn't she look like sunshine?" Truly, Alexa's face expressed such contentment and peace. She was a beautiful sight, but I just had to spoil it. I thought about how the goats butted one another, so I walked some distance away, lowered my head, and ran toward her as fast as I could, hitting her squarely in the chest. I literally knocked the wind out of her. Both our mothers were horrified and ran toward her. When I looked in Alexa's face, I saw no anger, just pain. In her suffering she tried to protect me from punishment and minimized the whole incident by saying, "I'm fine. Just fine. No need to worry."

Besides receiving a sound spanking, I had to kneel in the corner of the room for quite some time. I remember my back and knees hurting. Although the punishment did not cure me of my bad behavior, shame and remorse did fill my heart. There was no justification for my actions. The only thing that affected me was Alexa's ability to love and forgive me, even though I had hurt her so much. Now it reminds me of Jesus and His love for us. I believe I saw a glimpse of Him in her face and demeanor, and I'll never forget that day.

That summer was the last we would spend any time together. This poor widow and her sickly daughter took the train back to their village, but God cared for them. Sometime later Grandma Barbara married a village bachelor whom she had known a long time. The three of them ended up living happily together. In fact, years later when they found us through the International Red Cross, Grandma Barbara wrote to Mother, "Dear Dusia, if only I had lived as happily with your father for 20 days as I have with this man for 20 years." He was good to my aunt Alexa and treated her as if she were his own daughter. Later in life I mailed him two warm, flannel, checkered shirts, and he walked proudly, bragging to the villagers that "my granddaughter sent me these shirts." Maybe I made up a little for my meanness.

Spring came and went, and now summer brought many hot, sun-drenched days. But there was no rain. Our village, and the surrounding areas, began to experience drought. The fields, covered with golden wheat rippling like waves in the breeze, were almost ready to be harvested, but the soil was too dry. Unless a miracle happened, our survival was threatened. There was only one thing we knew to do: turn to God for help. We were deeply religious; no power on earth could shake our faith in God.

The priest and villagers decided to organize a procession to be led by the priest, who was clad in his glittering vestments and wore a golden miter on his head. In his left hand he carried a golden cross, and in his right, a censer full of burning frankincense. Assisting him was the deacon, dressed in black. Behind them a strong man hoisted aloft a large, golden cross that shone in the sun. Another man carried a banner depicting the virgin Mary holding Baby Jesus in her arms. Following them was the church choir singing in solemn, reverent tones. Old men and women, our parents, and we children joined the procession as it wound around the village and fields.

I don't remember how or why, but I was chosen to carry an icon, a gilded image of Christ. I carried that sacred relic in my hands, pressed it to my chest, and felt as if I were walking on clouds. I felt very privileged to play a part in that procession. I had seen grown-ups bow to other images in the church that depicted Mary holding Jesus tenderly in her arms and the angels hovering over Him with adoration. I began to feel as if He belonged to me exclusively, and I was filled with pride and joy. But I was confused about why this same Jesus, who was so adored, was also shown crucified in other pictures at church. This made my child's heart sad.

I wore a white dress fashioned from the remnants of a military parachute. When planes were shot down, our mothers would run out and gather the parachutes to make clothes for us. And when military trucks were attacked and bombed, we snatched the canvas from them, placed our feet on the material, traced around them with a pencil, and then cut out the pieces and sewed shoes. We also ate the military workhorses and cavalry mounts that had been killed.

As the procession continued singing and praying, I spotted Babushka Natasha watching me. "Doesn't she look like an angel?" I heard her say to a friend standing next to her. I lifted the icon heavenward with pride, and I felt as if my feet floated above the ground.

As the procession kept moving, we finally came to the banks of our river Torets. How we loved this river that flowed gently past our village and golden wheat fields. By now the water was shallow because of drought, but there was still enough for women to do their laundry, men to fish, the mill to grind grain into flour, and kids to splash to their hearts' content.

The priest stood there, surrounded by the elders and the softly singing church choir, imploring God for rain and for blessings on our labor. It came from a sincere heart, and we considered him a holy man, an intercessor between God and us villagers.

The day became hotter, and the sun stood in the middle of the sky. We all began experiencing hunger and thirst. But we had to go back to the church to return our items and say a final prayer before we could return home.

Back home we drank cool, fresh water from the well and ate our simple but tasty food. Mother fried potatoes and sausages in pork grease and served pickled cucumbers, tomatoes, and crunchy sauerkraut, with a slice of watermelon for dessert. And, of course, there was always homemade vodka. As evening brought cooler temperatures and time for singing and folk dancing, people would forget their troubles, if only for a few hours.

I know in my heart that God answered our prayers, because a few days later a gentle rain came that lasted long enough to sufficiently water our fields and save our crops. I also know that many a grandma kneeled before her icons that night and thanked God for His loving-kindness and answered prayers.

Not long after the drought I experienced my first village funeral. The man of the house died and was laid in a rough coffin, which was placed on the kitchen table. It was a hot day, the windows were open, and the flies were all drawn to the smell of death. No matter how many times the grown-ups waved off the flies, they kept landing on the deceased's face. A ribbon was placed on his forehead, and all of us stood in line to say our farewells and show respect by kissing him on the ribbon.

He was not a pretty sight—no makeup, no beautification. The reality and ugliness of death sobered us all, including us children. As men carried the casket to the cemetery, the poor grief-stricken widow, a black scarf covering her head, followed with her young children. But as the custom was, they hired a woman who, to me, seemed to make a lot of noise. As she beat her chest with a fist, she cried and wailed, "Oh, Timothy, why have you left the children and me? Who will take care of us now? How will I provide and raise these fatherless children all by myself? Oh, Timothy, why have you done this to us?"

Now all the women broke out, wailing loudly, as the woman continued to stir up everyone's emotions. What she cried about was real. Life was hard already, and losing a spouse was horrible—there was no life insurance and no social security or social services to depend upon. The poor widow was fully dependent on family and friends, but they themselves were barely managing to survive. Her only hope and trust would be in God.

But as I witnessed that scene and heard the lamenting, I became annoyed with the whole performance. It was so theatrical, and I felt that the hired mourner, who kept asking the dead man why he died, was putting a guilt trip on him. I felt sorry for him. He just got sick and died, but the hired mourner's own husband was alive and well, and I played with her children. And the worst part of the whole thing was that she would get paid for her performance. None of it made sense to me.

Soon after that memorable funeral, I found myself sitting on the front steps of our house. We were having a respite from the bombs and flying bullets, and the sun was shining brightly. Suddenly I heard yelling and screaming. As I turned to see what the commotion was all about, I caught sight of our widowed neighbor in the back of her house hanging onto her chicken by its legs while a young German soldier yanked on the poor creature's neck.

She was a stout woman in her 50s, and her arms were strong from physical labor. She was determined not to let go of her chicken. The tall, skinny young soldier in full uniform had only the strength of the shotgun that hung from his shoulder.

As they were tugging at the cackling creature, its feathers flying in all directions, its owner gave one last solid jerk and the hen was suddenly freed from the soldier's grasp. The woman wedged the hen protectively under her arm and marched off victoriously toward the barn, her head held high. The poor young man just stood there looking dejected. He would have felt even worse if he had understood all the unflattering names she called him in our language and the curses she had hurled at him. That day I learned an important lesson from the chicken and its owner: never give up.

Chickens seemed to be the center of many a controversy. Lydia, Mother's friend and roommate from trade school, who by now was married to Father's friend, Alex, was in her kitchen when several German soldiers barged in. They were hungry, so they made themselves comfortable at the kitchen table and demanded a nice dinner. Lydia tried to explain that her cupboards were empty and she had no food. One of the soldiers, who seemed to be the leader of the group, stood up and looked out the window. There he saw the neighbor's chickens roaming around and, pointing at them, said, "Go fetch one and prepare us dinner."

Lydia shook her head. "They are not mine," she said. The soldier removed his gun from its holster, set it on the table, and smiled smugly, "Now they are." The soldiers got their dinner.

Prepping a chicken for dinner is a memory I still carry with me. Mother would catch her victim, put its head on the chopping block (the same stump Alexa had sat on), and, with expert precision, chop its head off with the ax.

On one occasion the poor creature slipped out of Mother's grasp and started running around the yard as Mother, still holding the ax high in the air, charged after it. The headless chicken made a full circle and, not having eyes to see, headed straight into Mother's open arms. I literally saw a chicken running around with its head cut off!

Chapter 1

Because we had been blessed with rain, the crops were successful, and the villagers became very busy at harvesttime. Pigs were slaughtered and processed, debris was cleaned out of root cellars, barrels were taken out into the yard and scrubbed with scalding hot water to prevent spoilage of the new products that would be stored in them, and new sand was added to the cavities in the root cellars where potatoes, carrots, beets, and turnips were covered with sand to preserve their freshness.

Our root cellars became mini supermarkets. They were giant holes dug deep into the ground. Inside, we stored barrels of pickled tomatoes, sauerkraut mixed with sweet apples, and pickled cucumbers.

In addition, summer fruits were dried in the sun, and in winter we chewed them like candy or made fruit compote. Mushrooms strung on threads dangled from kitchen ceilings to dry over woodstoves, and braided garlic hung on the walls. Of course, we always had plenty of roasted sunflower and pumpkin seeds, sunflower oil, and occasionally even meat. All this "wealth" was produced by our hard labor and wonderful soil.

Millet and barley were thrashed, and we cooked them into hot cereals or soups. It was a busy time of preparation before we were covered by snow and frost. Winters in our country could be very harsh, and the men had to make sure we had enough chopped firewood for our stoves. We used the wood sparingly, just enough for kindling, because we were surrounded mostly by fields and not many woods. We also burned a cheap coal. To keep ourselves warm, we wore layers upon layers of clothing. We made strips out of rags and wrapped them around our feet to wear inside our *valenki* (boots made of wool felt). They felt very warm and cozy until we went outside. Then our feet became wet and frozen, since the *valenki* soaked up melted snow. We would hang the strips in front of the hot stove to dry, and then the process of getting wet, cold feet would start all over again.

After the fall harvests, winters were a little less busy and allowed us some time to socialize. Families and neighbors would visit one another, and the host would fry lots of potatoes in lard with onions and serve whole-wheat bread and pickles to complete the supper.

The men made their own vodka, which flowed freely, and depending on which army was occupying our area at the time, the soldiers enjoyed it as well. But it was a curse. We struggled enough with poverty as it was, and this only added more sorrow by creating drunken domestic violence and sending many homes up in flames—the stills were operated in the kitchens and required only a spark to set things ablaze.

One such winter evening we had company, and after a simple, filling meal, everyone started singing. They tried to outsing one another by competing to sing the highest note and hold it the longest. Mother was good at it, but so were the others, and the vodka seemed to give the contestants an advantage. As our guests began leaving, I climbed onto the table and collected the remaining drops of vodka from the various glasses into one glass, which made a nice sip. As I drank it, my throat and mouth burned like fire, and I crawled into bed before I could get in trouble. I slept soundly. In any event, winter began, and with such a bountiful harvest stored away, we were all set. Or so we thought.

Because of the heavy fighting constantly taking place in our area, we literally kept two armies fed, and stores of food began to dwindle quickly. It became scarce in the cities, and the people began coming to our village, begging for what little we now had in exchange for warm clothing. Woolen shawls, stockings, hats, mittens, sweaters, and *valenki* were much appreciated. We didn't care for their jewelry or fancy things. We needed practical things. And they were just as happy for a bag of carrots, potatoes, beets, or small bags of millet or barley.

Lydia, Mother's roommate from school, also came from the city with her son, Volodya. I was happy to have a little visitor almost the same age, as I was one month older than he. He was such a well-behaved boy, not like the wild boys from the village with whom I constantly fought for the fun of it, and I really liked him. Mother gave Lydia as much food as she could carry. In exchange I was gifted with Volodya's warm woolen sweater.

Once when Lydia came by herself, Mother gave her a sack of potatoes, which she carried on her back as she walked home to the city. As she was crossing over a brook on a small wooden bridge, the Russians and Germans started shooting at one another. Caught in the crossfire, she threw herself down on the bridge and the potatoes spilled out of the sack and rolled into the water below. We would laugh about this story for many years to come, but it was not funny then.

* * *

One cold winter morning, as Baba Maryna and I sat at the small kitchen table looking out the window, we saw snowflakes gently falling and birds hopping about the bare branches of the fruit trees. It was warm and cozy inside the house, and we could hear the fire crackling in the stove. She was shelling roasted sunflower seeds and collecting them for me in an empty matchbox. After a while Baba Maryna began to nod off and made her way to her bedroom for a nap. By this time we all knew that her health was beginning to fail.

I was bored and lonely until I looked out the window and saw my neighbor, Sonya, sliding on a frozen puddle with a visiting friend. I hurriedly put on my quilted coat, wrapped a shawl around my head, and ran out to join them. As I drew near, Sonya greeted me tersely. "Look, Alla, go home. We don't want you around here."

I was stunned. We had been playing together for as long as I could remember, and now she was humiliating me in front of her new friend.

A burning rage swept over me, and I stepped closer to her, speaking loudly enough for her friend to hear. "You know, Sonya, your mother has been running around with German soldiers."

The shock and hurt that registered on her face had the intended effect. She burst into tears and ran into her house with her friend trailing behind her. I marched back to my house, head held high. I was pleased with myself—but not for long. Mother burst into the house a little while later, her face twisted with fury. She grabbed my arm, spun me around, and yelled at the top of her lungs, "What is it you said about Sonya's mother?" She didn't wait for an answer, but gave me a sound spanking and pushed me into the corner of the room. "There, on your knees! And stay there until I tell you to get up!"

After a while my knees and back began to hurt, and my backside still burned—Mother's arm was strong. Now I was mad, not only at Sonya, but at Mother as well. She hadn't even asked for my side of the story. So I was still fuming and feeling sorry for myself when Babushka Natasha came to visit.

"Oh, what has our angel done?" she asked, seeing me kneeling in the corner.

"That's not an angel, that's a demon!" Mother retorted. "Do you realize what she said about Helen?"

Mother explained the situation, and I turned my head to see Babushka Natasha's reaction. She clasped her hands in shock, rolled her eyes toward heaven as if asking for God's mercy, and then she looked at me. Hurt and disappointment were written all over her face.

It was only then that I felt keen regret. I hadn't wanted to hurt her. I loved her too much and knew how much she loved me. I was also aware that what I had said in anger was not only a lie, but dangerous as well. The woman's character was spotless, and they were a happy family, but rumors like that could catch fire. If it reached the Soviet authorities, even just as gossip, she would be severely punished. After all, it was wartime.

That winter I was an outcast to my family and neighbors. Sonya wouldn't play with me anymore, and the other children shunned me. No one liked me, and even though I knew so little about Him, I was sure my only friend was God. As I ponder those long-ago years, I wonder how such a little girl could cause so much pain and, for one so young, show such a mean spirit. To this day I regret what I said.

But God in His mercy took pity on me in my loneliness that winter. A new family moved into the house on the other side of ours: a mother and father, a teenage son, and Zina, a girl a little younger and smaller than I. Since she was new to our village, she looked up to me, and I once again felt needed and important. She had a small face and large, expressive brown eyes that peered at everything as though she was in constant wonder. Her hair was short and looked as though a comb had never touched it. She looked like a little elf, and I loved her. Besides, she was lively and fun. Winter was still with us, and we enjoyed sledding down the gentle slopes of the banks of the river Torets onto the frozen river, making sure to avoid the steep and dangerous areas where people had been known to fall to their deaths.

One day the two of us had to visit the outhouse. It was dark inside and the hole large, so I hesitated to climb on top, but not that wiggly Zina. "Oh, Alla, you are such a scaredy-cat!" she laughed. "Look at me!" In no time she climbed up, slipped, and fell in. Luckily, almost everything inside was frozen solid. I bent over to look down at her and there she lay, wailing loudly. I'll never forget the comical sight of Zina sprawled out wearing a boot on one foot and a shoe on the other.

I ran to her mother, yelling, "Auntie! Auntie! Zina fell into the outhouse!" Zina's mother reacted quickly. She grabbed a rope and pail, ran to the outhouse, lifted the lid, and lowered down the pail. Zina climbed into the pail and was pulled up.

It was a happy ending, except we had no running water, no detergents, and no disinfectants. Again, her mother knew what to do. She melted lots of snow and used strong alkali, but it took several days for Zina to become odor-free. I felt sorry for her and was happy to have her back. But our new neighbors didn't stay long. They soon moved to the city, and I truly missed her.

The fighting around our village became heavy that winter. The Germans still occupied our area, but the Russians were closing in. In fact, soldiers from both sides occupied the same abandoned factory, but in opposite wings, trying to stay warm. One Russian soldier who had been staying at our house told my father one evening that as it was getting dark and he was returning to his unit, he unwittingly approached the enemy's side of the factory. A German soldier spotted him and said, "Comrade, your unit is at the other end."

"If it wasn't for the war," said the Russian soldier to my father, "I would have invited that guy to dinner and treated him to a bottle of vodka. He could have shot me, but he didn't."

The Germans were well equipped and more prepared for the war than either the Russians or Ukrainians. They had white, snowsuit-like outfits that blended well with the snow, and their casualties were fewer. However, despite their advantage in arms and equipment, they were met by fierce resistance.

As the war continued, the Germans were pushed back again, and now it was the Soviets who occupied our village. Bullets were constantly whistling over our heads, and explosions lit the sky. Our only hiding place was the root cellar across the yard from our house. Many a night wounded soldiers were brought into our cellar, pleading for help, but my parents had no medicine or bandages. We were all so desperately poor and helpless.

One night as the battle started raging again, this time more fiercely than ever, Mother ran from our root cellar to the house, ducking bullets, to check on Baba Maryna, who was sick. We couldn't keep her in the damp, cold cellar, so she stayed in the house alone. But she had developed a fever and had begun to hallucinate. "Dusia," she said to my mother, "go to the gate and let the shepherd and his sheep in." There was no gate, and Mother knew the end was near. She gave Baba Maryna a sponge bath, wrapped her in a thick, warm comforter, and placed her on the living room floor so that she wouldn't roll out of her bed.

The next morning a young, freckle-faced soldier with an ashen face banged on our root-cellar door and lifted it open. "*Towarischt!*" he yelled. "You have a dead woman in your house! We came during the night, and I felt a blanket on the floor, so I pulled it to cover myself. In the morning I woke up to find this old dead woman staring at me. She scared me more than all the flying bullets! To think I slept with her all night!"

Father found some scrap planks of wood and fashioned a crude coffin while Mother wrapped Baba Maryna in that same comforter the soldier had shared with her. She looked so small as they laid her in that box. Father, Mother, and even this poor soldier, who appeared to be a strong farmboy, hacked a hole into our frozen backyard, and that's where we buried her.

Another day, two cold, ragged young soldiers climbed down into our cellar. Wearing ill-fitting uniforms, they looked like rosy-cheeked boys just out of high school. One had a bandage on his head through which blood was seeping. He was shaking uncontrollably, crying, "Mama, Mama!" His friend explained that a bomb had exploded close to them and sent him into shock.

Our hearts were sad for these two lost-looking boys who were attempting to defend us from the Nazis, and Mother, possessing no medical supplies, decided she could at least feed them. When there was a lull in the shooting, she ran to the house to boil potatoes on the woodstove and brought them back to the cellar along with dried bread. We also had pickled cucumbers and slices of *salo* (salted, raw pig fat) that were already in the cellar.

After resting and being fed, the wounded soldier regained his composure, and Mother filled their pockets with leftover potatoes and dried bread before they left in the morning.

About a week after we buried Baba Maryna, the battle continued fiercely and the whistling bullets and explosions increased in intensity. In the middle of the night our neighbor knocked on our cellar door and shouted, "Nikolai! Nikolai! Your house is on fire!"

We quickly climbed up the ladder and crawled out of our hiding place, only to be met by the sight of our house ablaze. Mother and Father took me by the hands and ran, the ice and snow crunching under our feet. I turned my head to look back at our home for the last time and saw the flames dancing on the thatched roof Father had so lovingly fashioned. My heart ached.

With the moon and stars lighting our way, we hurried through the crossfire to Babushka Natasha and Grandpa Anton's house, which was less than a mile away. We were shivering with cold and out of breath as we knocked on their door. Wordlessly they took us in. This would be our home now.

loved living at Babushka Natasha's house. She and Grandpa Anton loved me unconditionally, and I got to sleep on their pallet right next to Babushka Natasha, her arms holding me securely each night.

Spring brought warmth, and the river Torets began to thaw. With the sun beating down on the snow, the water churned and the riverbank overflowed, flooding half our yard. Even though we had lost our house, the garden was intact, and the land still belonged to us. As the water receded, many stranded fish flopped about on the ground, so Mother and the other women collected them. The fish ended up in frying pans, and we also feasted on tasty fish soup consisting of fish bones and heads cooked with carrots and onions. Nothing went to waste.

One spring day Mother took me to our old place so she could work in the garden. Content to bask in the sunshine, I seated myself on the foundation, which was all that was left of our house. While Mother was digging in the soil, I was horrified to see Sonya's mother walking toward me. I hung my head in shame and didn't dare look up at her. How well I remembered my ugly outburst.

"Oh, Alla," I heard her begin, "you have grown. You are such a big girl now."

Her voice and smiling face told me that I was forgiven. How I admired her for her kind and generous words, a wonderful example of the forgiveness we can find in God. I shyly smiled back and watched her approach my mother. I listened to them chatting away and laughing. As a result of my vindictiveness, their relationship had been strained as well.

We continued to live with my grandparents throughout that summer. One day Mother went to the farmer's market in the city to sell some of our produce. Many people came to her stand, including Zina's mother. She was so thin that Mother hardly recognized her.

"Dusia," she began, "do you remember my little Zina?"

Mother nodded.

"Well, she is dead! We were sitting at the supper table during a thunderstorm when all of a sudden she was struck by lightning that came through the window. She fell off her chair dead!"

Mother clasped her hands in shock and sorrow, and then both women hugged one another and cried. That little Zina had been my ray of sunshine that winter, and I had truly loved her.

At that time our village was occupied by the Germans, so we were allowed to attend church service. It was summer, and Babushka Natasha was busy, so I went to church all by myself. I loved the house of God. It was like stepping into another world with the colorful pictures of angels, saints, and the virgin Mary and Jesus with gilded halos surrounding me. The priest chanted solemnly in a singsong voice at the altar, and the choir sang reverently.

But one Sunday was extra-special: a wedding celebration in which the bride was dressed in a long, white dress and veil. I don't remember the groom, but I thought the bride to be the most gorgeous thing I had ever seen.

Now I wanted to be a bride too. Sometime later I enlisted two neighbor boys to help with my wedding ceremony. They were hesitant at first, but I promised each of them a luscious apple from Babushka Natasha's apple tree. They couldn't resist. No one was home, so I took down one of Babushka Natasha's dining-room curtains, tied a knot at one end, and put it on my head. I dragged the boys into the bushes so we wouldn't be seen, and ordered the more presentable one to kneel next to me while the other acted as our officiating priest. He mimicked the priest's deep voice, pretended to wave a censer, and then pronounced us husband and wife.

I kept my promise and gave them their apples as they took off.

Just then Babushka Natasha came home. I could see disappointment written all over her face when she saw me.

"Babushka Natasha, look at me!" I beamed. "I just got married!"

"Take that curtain off your head and hang it back where it belongs!" she ordered.

I did as I was told. She seemed to like it a lot better on her window than on my head, and even though I was a little disappointed, the desire to be a bride never left me.

Chapter **13**

About a week later, during a lull in the shooting, Mother decided to take me on a train ride to another town to visit her half brother, Peter, and his family. It was very exciting to ride the train, see the blue sky, and watch miles and miles of golden yellow wheat fields rippling in the breeze like the waves of an ocean. Every now and then we passed a small village. The little thatch-roofed houses were surrounded by a variety of flowers, such as roses, lilacs, hollyhocks, and sunflowers so large and tall they made the houses look smaller yet. Also surrounding the homes were various fruit trees and gardens. Back home we children would climb the apple, pear, apricot, and cherry trees and eat those juicy sweet fruits without needing to wash them first. We also had rows and rows of corn, which was very tasty. No pesticides endangered us. Our soil was so rich and fertile we could grow anything and everything by just adding water.

We finally arrived at our destination and began the long walk to the village where our relatives lived. There were no telephones, taxis, or cars. The sun was beating down on our heads, and blisters began developing on my heels. My shoes were always either too big or too small, squeezing my toes or flapping, having been handed down from someone else who had outgrown them. Either way, I suffered, and we had no money to buy new ones. On top of it all, I was getting thirsty. I longed for a glass of cool water; I'm sure Mother did, too.

"How much farther to their village, Mama?" I wailed.

"Not much, *Allachka*. Just hang on."

And so I did. There was nothing else we could do but continue our walk.

At first the road was winding, but then it straightened out, and finally we saw the village in the distance. How happy we were! We could see the sides of the road lined with wildflowers, such as red clover, chicory, Queen Anne's lace, sweet peas, and poppies. Ukrainian girls would pluck them and fashion wreaths to adorn their heads. On both sides of the road were fields of ripe, yellow grain beneath the blue sky, which is how our Ukrainian flag was designed: the top half sky blue, the bottom half golden yellow.

Since Uncle Peter had been expecting us, he was out on the road watching for his sister and little niece. He was tall and friendly. Because he had grown up on the farm, his muscles bulged. He wore the blue pants made of very sturdy flax typically worn by our men, which were almost like denim, and an untucked white linen shirt. What I remember most about him was his smile and how joyfully he picked me up. He was so strong I thought he would squeeze me to death.

His wife, Helen, came running out, wiping her hands on her apron. "Where are those hungry boys?" she inquired, looking around. "You can't find them even with a lit candle!"

But it took only a few minutes for my cousins to show up. Their faces were dirty and sweaty from playing, but they were beaming with happiness at meeting their girl cousin. These boys were about 9 and 11 years of age and were eager to impress their little visitor with their antics.

While the table was being set and the grown-ups exchanged family news, my cousins invited me into their backyard, which was enclosed by a wooden picket fence and was where the turkeys were kept. The boys opened the gate ever so slowly, sneaked inside, and started teasing the turkeys by making faces and lots of trilling noises at the poor creatures. Immediately the turkeys inflated their necks and charged at them, but the boys climbed over the fence out of the turkeys' reach. I was impressed until their father came and yelled at them. Then they looked like little boys again.

When we finally went inside and washed up, we were invited to the table. Their home was simple, as was everyone else's, and contained handmade wood furniture. The table and chairs were large and sturdy, and a colorfully embroidered linen tablecloth brightened the house. Our dishes and spoons were carved out of wood.

I was assigned a seat between my cousins, and as we ate I couldn't take my eyes off Aunt Helen. She was such a pretty young woman with dark eyes, perfectly arched eyebrows, and beautiful, even white teeth. Her hair was braided and arranged in a coronet. I also noticed that she was much younger than Uncle Peter, how gently they treated one another, and how adoringly he looked at her.

We were served the traditional borscht, a typical Ukrainian soup consisting of cabbage, beets, carrots, potatoes, tomatoes, and peppers. First a chicken or a piece of beef is put into the pot, and vegetables are stirred in later. To top it off, fresh crushed garlic and dill straight from the garden are added. Aunt Helen ladled this wonderful soup into bowls and added dollops of homemade sour cream. Of course, along with that a slice of homemade whole-wheat bread with smooth, churned butter spread on top was served.

But a meal wouldn't be a meal without *vareniki*. A Ukrainian version of ravioli, our *vareniki* were made of dough shaped in large half-moon pockets, and filled with a variety of things, such as mashed potato, farmer cheese, or sauerkraut. During the summer, the *vareniki* were often filled with cherries, plums, or strawberries. They were boiled in water until the dough was tender and steaming, and served with butter and fried onions (not the fruit-filled ones), and topped with sour cream. Oh, how tasty!

Next we were served boiled sweet pumpkin mashed with cooked millet and butter, and slices of watermelon for dessert. Later in the afternoon we were given roasted sunflower and pumpkin seeds to snack on, all from their own garden.

After a very pleasant evening, it was time to go to sleep. Lots of clean, fresh straw was piled up on the dirt floor and a homemade linen bedsheet spread on top, and my cousins and I slept side by side on this and were covered with another linen sheet. Since the day had been exciting and tiring, I slept soundly. But then, to my horror, I wet the bed! When we woke up, the telltale dark spot staining the dirt floor was visible.

How loving the grown-ups were, and the cousins didn't make fun of me. In fact, everyone tried to console me, but in my imagination I was sure that by now the whole village knew about my mishap and that even the turkeys were laughing at me. But I also remember the love and compassion everyone showed, for they knew how humiliated I felt. Somehow it reminds me how tenderly our heavenly Father treats us when we mess up.

Many years later, shortly before Mother died, we were reminiscing about our lives in the Ukraine, and I surprised her by telling her how well I remembered our stay at her brother's home. She thought I had forgotten about it because I had been so young. She then told me about Uncle Peter's first wife and their failed marriage.

Apparently Grandpa Gregory had invited his friend from a neighboring village for dinner one evening and, as the custom was, for a few drinks of homemade vodka. Both men were considered hardworking and resourceful, and Gregory's friend was in a position to offer a nice dowry along with his pretty daughter. Therefore, these two men decided to marry Uncle Peter to the unsuspecting girl. What they didn't know was that she was already in love with someone else. But even if her father had known, he had the final say, and she had no choice but to obey.

The day for the wedding was set, and both villages partook in the celebration. Since it took place during harvesttime, there was plenty of fresh food, and a few animals were slaughtered for the occasion. Every household contributed from the abundance and generosity of their hearts. And, of course, there was much drinking to quench the men's "thirst."

Everyone was happy except the bride. Nevertheless, she did bring into the family a beautiful lacquered hope chest, artfully painted and filled with linens, a down comforter, pillows, and other goods. And so they were married.

Fall arrived, quickly followed by winter. There was always lots of work to be done on the farm, and the young wife performed her chores dutifully and got along with her in-laws. But spring arrived and everything changed.

Easter was nearing, and people were getting ready not only for planting but also celebrating spring and, most important, commemorating with great festivity and joy the resurrection of Jesus.

Because of our Greek Orthodox religion, we first abstained from eating meat for six weeks, substituting fish for the meat, and offered many prayers before icons. Finally the "Day of Resurrection" came. The villagers dressed in their cleanest and finest colorful outfits: intricately hand-embroidered blouses for the women and girls, and embroidered collars and cuffs for the men. The well-to-do shared sausages, hams, *paskas*, and eggs with the poorer villagers. The *paskas*, round sweetbreads with raisins, were placed in baskets lined with embroidered doilies. Brightly painted eggs, called *pysanky*, some with very intricate designs, were arranged around the *paskas*. Even today priests bless the *paskas* and *pysanky* by sprinkling "holy water" on them with sprigs of hyssop while the church choir sings.

When Saturday evening arrived and the services at church began, the congregation gathered inside. As always, the women and children stood on the left and the men on the right, everyone holding a lighted candle. The gilded icons glittered in the flickering candlelight while the mitered priests, with their long, bushy beards, looked very solemn and reverent as they performed the ceremonial rites and waved their smoke-filled censers. The balcony choir harmonized like angels from heaven.

At exactly midnight the church bells rang and the congregation went outside and walked around the church. Carrying a cross and censer, the priest led the procession and was followed by the singing choir. Church bells from neighboring villages blended beautifully with ours and, under the moonlit sky and shining stars, made for a magical evening.

When the procession ended, everyone broke out in joyous exclamation, "Christ is risen!" Family, friends, and strangers embraced and kissed one another three times on the cheek with tears of joy in their eyes, responding, "Truly, Christ is risen!" All barriers in rank, age, and gender were broken down for that evening. These were the types of joyous days we experienced before the long arm of Moscow reached our villages.

My mother had come to church with Peter's wife that evening. At the end of the procession, in the dark of night, Mother saw her kissing a young man, and it was not an "Easter kiss." My mother was 13 years old at the time, and with a broken heart she ran home and told Peter and her parents what she had seen. No sooner had she finished her story when Peter's wife burst through the door in tears and fell on her knees before her husband and in-laws. She begged them to release her from her marriage. She realized she didn't love Peter—she was in love with another man. Her request was granted immediately.

However, my mother could not tolerate such insult to her brother. She found the biggest and sharpest nail in the house and attacked the hope chest, gouging it and scratching all the designs beyond recognition. The poor bride was devastated. Even Mother regretted her evil deed in years to come.

But the story didn't end there. Not long afterward the poor, former daughter-in-law came back, fell on her knees again, and begged for forgiveness, asking to be reinstated in their home. The young man she loved had changed his mind. He didn't want a "used woman" and had disappeared.

"No, daughter," replied Grandpa Gregory, "you go back to your home. You humiliated our son and brought shame on our family. You don't belong here anymore."

It took several years for Uncle Peter to recover from this horrible blow, but he finally fell in love with Helen, a younger woman with a sweet and gentle disposition. Mother said they were very happy together, and their union produced my boy cousins.

Eventually, Uncle Peter's first wife realized that she actually did love him. He was a decent young man, and they could have lived happily together, but it was too late. Later she married an alcoholic widower with several children and was physically abused.

Mother was angry at Grandpa Gregory and his friend and concluded that those two old fools had ruined the poor girl's life.

By this time the Soviets had pushed the Nazis back and were occupying our area again. Our churches were locked up once more, and many of our people were arrested by the Soviets for having been too friendly with the Germans. Most of the time, however, they were just falsely accused by someone who wished them harm. The stress of living on the warfront caused us all to be suspicious of one another, and all trust was gone.

After several weeks the Nazis returned, but realizing they were losing the war, they began retreating for the last time. On their way out, they blew up railroads, factories, hospitals, government buildings, and took with them anything and everything of value. They even loaded trains with our rich, black soil and carted it off. We were amazed, for we thought everyone had the same wonderful soil we had.

At the beginning of the war, when we first heard rumors that the Germans were coming, we were excited, believing they would free us from the oppressive Soviet regime. But instead they forcefully took our greatest treasure with them, our able-bodied men, women, and youth, to be used for physical labor.

Some youth, who were looking for adventure, had previously volunteered to go. But mostly, the Nazis went door to door, checking for able bodies to work in their munitions factories, and ordered us to appear at the railroad stations at a specified date and time. The Nazis could see people were not happy about leaving their elderly parents to fend for themselves, their homes and farm animals, so to placate us, they promised us jobs and a place to live. With unspoken threats looming over us, we had no choice but to obey and go.

Babushka Natasha and Grandpa Anton brought my parents and me to the railroad station in a horse-drawn wagon. When the time came to say goodbye, my babushka put her arms around me and whispered, "I will wet your pillow with my tears, my precious little star." I was her only grandchild. I remember, though, my only wish was that she would let go of me, because I was so excited about riding on the train. I never saw her again. I didn't know it would be the last time we would say goodbye, but her words stayed with me forever.

The train was very crowded, and the three of us sat down when we finally found unoccupied seats. There was nothing else to do other than observe the people or look out the windows and watch the villages pass by as our train rushed toward Germany and an unknown future.

I noticed on the train many teenage boys and girls who didn't look happy. They had been torn away from their families against their will. As the sun began setting behind the horizon, several of the youth stood up and went to the platform in the back of the train. I don't think anybody else but me thought anything of it. The rest probably figured the teenagers had gotten tired of sitting and needed some fresh air. But as the train came to a bend and started slowing down, all of a sudden several of them jumped off the train one at a time, rolled down the embankment, and started running toward the thickets and into the forest. We heard shots and cursing from the German guards on the train and then the distant cries of the wounded teenagers. We all sat quietly, absorbed in our own thoughts, as the train picked up speed. We knew someone's sons and daughters, wounded and bleeding, were dying out there with no one to wipe their tears or soothe their pain. The night came, but it was a restless one.

After several days of slow travel, we finally arrived in Germany and stayed in the city of Dresden for three months. What living conditions we experienced, I do not recall. Mother said it was very crowded. I only remember that it was an incredibly beautiful city. I saw houses with balconies full of colorful flowers and window baskets overflowing with even more flowers, manmade ponds with water lilies, and the people, especially women, beautifully dressed. Coming from a poor village, I was in awe, seeing for the first time men dressed in well-tailored suits and nice shoes, and women fashionably dressed and coiffed. I later read that Dresden, once a medieval city, was a cultural mecca with many historical buildings and museums housing famous works of art. But the city was destroyed during the bombardments by the Allies, along with many treasures of art and life. Years later I learned that the destruction was unnecessarily severe because there were no military installations located in Dresden.

Escorted by Nazi guards, we took a train to Leipzig and then were transported by military trucks to a camp outside the city limits. It was the summer of 1942 when we arrived at our final destination and were placed in barracks. We could still smell the fresh paint. The barbed-wire fence was shiny with a large, single-lock gate, and guards with shotguns and German shepherds by their sides watched over us. It finally dawned on us—we were in a forced-labor camp, not free, but prisoners. Labels with the letters "OST" fastened to the left side of our coats meant we were from the "east," Slavs from Slavic countries.

Early each morning our parents were picked up by trucks and transported to work in factories. Mother worked in a laboratory department as a chemistry technician where they were attempting to improve the quality of cement mix, and Father labored at a parts factory for military vehicles. They would be returned late every night, exhausted.

We children were left in the camp under the supervision of a woman who really had no control over us. We ran wild, beating one another up with sticks and stones and playing war games, pretending to be Germans and Americans at war.

One day soon after we arrived, we children lingered at the barbed-wire fence and watched trucks bringing in many loads of building materials, mostly planks and beams. As the structures went up, we realized more barracks were being built, also with barbed-wire fencing around them. But the fence between us and the new camp remained.

We didn't have to wonder long who it was for. Soon we saw lines of prisoners escorted into the new camp. We could see their tattered uniforms, some limping and supported by their comrades, others with bandages on their heads or arms in slings. As those poor men moved slowly and painfully, they were kicked and punched by the guards for no reason at all. Once they were installed into their new quarters, I remember those prisoners coming to their side of the fence and trying to talk to us children. We didn't know who they were and couldn't understand what they were saying, so we would just rush by them. They were unshaven and their hair was matted, but they smiled at us and seemed friendly.

We couldn't understand why the guards were so hateful to them. After a while some of our grown-ups solved the mystery. The prisoners were Italian soldiers who refused to fight against the Americans as the war was coming to an end. They didn't want to fight and die for "Il Duce" Mussolini. Considered traitors, they had been captured by the Germans and treated cruelly.

One day as we were outside running around and playing games, we saw a handsome young man in a brown shirt, a swastika band wrapped around his left arm. He was muscular and in good physical shape, and his boots were polished to a shine. Next to him was his companion, a German shepherd. His fur brushed to a shine, he too appeared well groomed. The way his master smiled at him and stroked him, while the dog responded to him by happily wagging his tail, was a picture of serenity. Within a few minutes, though, the scene changed abruptly as the same handsome young man began yelling at and punching an Italian prisoner. We children watched in horror as the prisoner lay on the ground, crying and begging for the beating to stop. After that incident took place, nothing shocked us anymore—we aged that day and lost the innocence of our childhood.

Chapter **15**

Early during our imprisonment our parents were given Sundays off from work, and we were actually allowed to leave the camp to visit parks and even a zoo. But soon after, as the Allies began directing their nightly air raids toward our area, our freedom and food supply became more restricted. We were beginning to feel hunger acutely, and with hunger came weight loss. I remember that Mother brought a chunk of salt from the factory, and I sat and licked it, crying because I was so hungry.

We were sharing a corner room in a barrack with another family much like ours. The young couple, Boris and Tina, had a daughter younger than I, and were from Ukraine as well. It was a small room, but we had bunk beds. We girls slept on the upper beds while our parents squeezed together on the lower ones.

Boris was a tall, very energetic man. He was always bragging about his escapades back home, such as stealing, but somehow never got caught and, thus, escaped punishment. He told us all about his experiences with great relish and pride.

One day Boris had something important to share with my parents. "Listen, Nick," he said to my father, half whispering, "some of my friends and I have got a plan. You see that German farmer coming in and out of the shed on his potato field carrying something? Bet he's got a root cellar in there full of food. We are going to sneak out and investigate, and you are welcome to join us."

"How will we get there?" my father asked. "The fence is tall, and we are surrounded by guards and dogs."

"We have it all figured out, my friend," Boris answered smugly. "We'll dig a tunnel under the fence. The next thing you know, we'll be on the other side."

Father hesitated, looking at Mother. She did not discourage him. The hunger pangs were acute for all of us. They were also thinking of me because I was skin and bones at this point.

Father agreed, and everything went as planned. They dug the tunnel and made it into the field one night, then into the shed, not realizing the guards followed them every step of the way. They were caught and brought back to the barrack, and their names were written down. A few days went by as though nothing had happened, but my father knew it was not over yet. He shared his fears and forebodings with Mother.

One night Mother had a nightmare, which she shared with Tina, who claimed to know how to interpret dreams.

"Tell me, Dusia, what was your dream about?" she asked.

"Well," said Mother, "I was carrying a large, heavy black cross on my back. I came to a chair and was supposed to step up onto a table and reach the nail on the wall to hang the cross, but as I tried to do this, the table collapsed under me, and I fell through it with my cross."

"Oh, Dusia," said Tina sadly. "All through your life you will be carrying a heavy cross. You will suffer much."

Mother was already suffering, and she, too, had a bad feeling about the future.

My eighth birthday soon arrived, and Mother took me to the factory with her where her German women coworkers wanted to meet me. The women were friendly and gave me some cookies, and at the end of the day we came back to our room at the camp. We were met by a teary-eyed Tina and two other women.

"Oh, Dusia!" cried Tina. "They came and arrested our husbands and took them away in a car to who knows where!"

Mother was stunned, and I was crushed by the knowledge that my father was gone. How well I remember that day. We knew what our men did was wrong, and now we were all paying for it. But the punishment was greater than the crime. It was intended to be a lesson to the rest of the prisoners in our camp.

Mother asked our camp leader where the men were taken. He was not a kind man, but somehow Mother managed to gain permission and a paper allowing us to take a streetcar to the place where prisoners were held before being transported to Buchenwald concentration camp.

We found the place. It looked like a huge warehouse with no rooms, just an open space with rows and rows of triple-high bunk beds and men lying motionless on them.

A guard escorted us as we walked down row after row, searching the faces of those poor men. There was no spark of life or glimmer of hope in their eyes, just empty stares. They looked like cattle headed for slaughter.

How we longed to see my father just one more time, give him a hug and a kiss, and tell him how much we loved him. But before we had a chance to see the rest of the prisoners, the accompanying guard ran out of time and patience and ordered us to return to our camp.

Tina became depressed, and as days turned into weeks, this small woman began to look like a helpless child. She lost her will to live. But not Mother; she was a fighter. She continued to work, shared her tears and sorrows with her coworkers, and received lots of sympathy.

Several weeks later, as the nightly raids intensified, we lost Tina and her daughter in the fiery inferno the fateful night she refused to run for shelter.

That night as we stumbled into the shelter, which was simply a large, sturdy underground hole lined with bricks, we found it already packed with other prisoners—Russian and Ukrainian civilians as well as the Italian soldiers, who had been placed separately at the rear of the bunker.

Smoke from the burning barracks began seeping in, making it difficult to breathe, and a young Nazi soldier stationed at the door threatened to shoot us if we moved. We were trapped.

I watched curiously the reactions of those around me. Some people sobbed quietly, resigned to certain death. Others wore hateful expressions, cursed the Germans, and tensely watched the soldier with the gun in his hand.

A teenage girl cried, "Mother, why did you give birth to me? I didn't ask to be born into this cruel world!" A middle-aged man snapped at her, "Shut up! You'll scare the little one!" and pointed at me. Even though I was only 8 years old, I felt sorry for the girl, who was simply an older but still frightened child.

Another group knelt in a circle and prayed. My heart leaped with joy because I finally saw people who hadn't given up hope. In the middle of the circle, a man lifted his hands toward heaven and pleaded in Russian, "O dear God, please save us! Hear our prayers and help us."

Our situation seemed hopeless. Gasping for air, we desperately needed to escape the thick, black smoke, but the Nazi continued to block the door. "You move, and I'll shoot you!" he shouted. But we could see that he, too, feared for his life.

No sooner did the praying man say "Amen" than suddenly, as though an unseen power lifted us simultaneously to our feet, we all surged forward and ran out of the bunker, knocking down the guard and trampling him before he could pull the trigger.

Eyewitnesses later told us that when the Italian prisoners behind us tried to escape, other guards rushed over and shot at them, bolting the door before they could get out. With no way out, they died from smoke inhalation.

As we dashed toward the camp's only gate, the crowd pressed around me so tightly that I was carried forward even though my feet were barely touching the ground. Mother managed to keep hold of my hand and pulled me to safety. But when we reached the gate, we found that it was locked. The constant barrage of bombs rained down burning debris and shrapnel on us. Our clothes caught fire, and people screamed in fear and pain. It was truly a Red Sea experience. From a human perspective there was no escape—we would certainly perish—but God watched over us. Frantically we pushed against the gate until it gave way, and we surged out of the burning camp into the open fields where we collapsed, dazed and panting, sucking the cool, fresh air into our lungs.

It was then I wondered who this great God was who had answered those people's prayers. How could He have heard their prayers when He lived so far away in my grandmother's village church? Confused and filled with questions, I comforted myself with the thought that someday, when I grew up, I would find God.

The guards soon came to reclaim those of us who had survived the destruction of the camp and who had not been trampled to death in the melee at the gate. Shivering with cold from the early-morning chill, we were given blankets and loaded into covered military trucks to be transported to a partially abandoned factory in downtown Leipzig. Several hundred of us had survived, and we now slept on the concrete floor of the still functional three-story brick building.

In a way it was a blessing that our camp had burned down. We children quickly discovered that the local civilians, passing by on their way to work, carried little brown bags—food! Early each morning we would line up along the brick walls of the factory and watch them walk by. We were a pitiful sight: skinny, ragged, filthy, starved, and lice-infested. Their hearts went out to us, and they shared with us their sandwiches, and sometimes even a hard-boiled egg. This continued throughout the summer, and we actually enjoyed our stay in the factory.

Another bright spot in my life at that time was Nicky, an 8-month-old baby boy who slept with his mother next to where Mother and I slept. He had a round, chubby, smiling face, blue eyes, and blond hair. He was such a happy child, and I loved playing with him. In the mornings I would wake up to find him sitting on his thin mattress, watching me and waiting for me to open my eyes. Still half asleep, I would stretch out my arms and pull him to me, and there we would lie, happy to be together while his mother slept soundly with her back turned to us. But after a while he would grow restless and crawl back to his mother. I knew he was getting hungry, for it was feeding time, and only she could satisfy his hunger. As for me, it was time to watch the local people walk to work.

One morning when I woke up, Nicky wasn't waiting for me. It was eerily quiet except for a few coughs here and there from those sick with colds or tuberculosis. Mother had already gone to work, and all I saw was Nicky's mother's back as she slept. I figured he was still asleep, too, so I rushed out to find some breakfast. As I returned from begging, I was met by two soldiers, one carrying little Nicky's body and the other leading his mother by the arm. She was crying, but I did not detect real sorrow or heartbreak in her voice. It was obvious, even to me, that she was faking her grief. Rumor had it that she had suffocated her son with a pillow. He had been born out of wedlock, and her new boyfriend didn't want Nicky around. The war desensitized many people, and they became cruel.

Ever an efficient and hardworking people, the Germans soon built a new labor camp for us farther away from the city than the previous camp. Mother and I were moved into a tiny room of our own. Our next-door neighbors were a single mother and her three children. The oldest girl, Raya, was my age and had two younger brothers. Because the walls were so thin, we could hear the boys crying every night, "Mommy, I'm hungry! Give me something to eat!" But there was no food. Each day we were given one slice of dark bread with a little butter and a very smelly, watery turnip soup that tasted like dirty dishwater. The occasional piece of potato was highly prized. Mother would always tell me, "Chew slowly, and don't run. That way you'll conserve energy and you won't get hungry so quickly."

Things went from bad to worse, and we were desperately hungry. Once Mother brought a few handfuls of cement mix from the factory where she worked. The mix contained potato starch as one of the ingredients. After building a makeshift stove by stacking bricks with a sheet of metal placed on top and building a small fire beneath it, she added water to the mix, shaped it into patties, and fried them on the sheet for us to eat. As I tried to eat them, I could feel the gritty texture of the cement grinding against my teeth. To this day I have never been a picky eater.

The camp director was a stocky man in his 40s whom we called "Nero," and the name was a perfect fit. He had a large head that sat on a short neck, his face was always twisted with hatred, and the three middle fingers on his right hand were missing. He would wave that hand under people's noses and declare that he had lost them in a Russian prison camp. We didn't know if it was true or not, but he certainly used this as an excuse to abuse the adult prisoners.

Day after day our parents, returning hungry and exhausted from their work in military factories, would be greeted at the gate by Nero, who was dressed in his brown, woolen military uniform and swastika band and was surrounded by guards and dogs. Completely unprovoked, he would kick and punch our parents and then laugh with evil glee. We often wondered if he was mentally unbalanced. We children would huddle together, attempting to comfort one another. Witnessing these cruel, ugly scenes, we felt sorry for our parents but couldn't help, so we just silently wept. There was nowhere to go for help, and no tolerance for complaint.

We communicated with Nero through a translator who spoke broken Russian. She was a German woman with sharp features and listless brown hair who dressed in a skirted military uniform. She would always translate in a way that infuriated Nero even more, and foam would spray from his mouth as he screamed and waved his disfigured hand at us. The translator would then step back with a smug smile. We knew she had translated inaccurately to get us in trouble, and it seemed to give her some kind of twisted satisfaction.

But not everyone was mean-spirited. There was one well-liked guard who never abused us, and whenever he witnessed Nero's behavior, we saw a pained expression on his face.

The feelings of helplessness and hopelessness were overwhelming because there was nowhere to go to ask for help or protection. Even though we felt forsaken by God and man, I know God still watched over us. Many German men from the local villages would come to our barbed-wire fence and bring us food. It wasn't much, for they had very little themselves, and there were so many of us. But it touched our hearts to watch them risk arrest or gunshots from the guards. We were, after all, the enemy.

I remember one man in particular named Max. He was a short gentleman in his 50s who had a small tuft of blond hair on top of his balding head. He came regularly and brought a pink-colored pudding for me only. I always saw compassion in his friendly smile. Sympathy came from this man who had lost his only child in the war and whose wife had left him.

The courage and care of these people warmed our hearts and lifted our morale. It was as if God were saying, "You are not alone; I care about you," and we felt there was still some good left in this dark, painful world.

Raya and I became very close friends because we were the same age. We were so close, in fact, that we contracted German measles at the same time. An epidemic among the workforce in our camp was unwanted, so we were transported to a hospital and given medical attention in the city of Leipzig. We even shared the same room.

As always, the nightly air raids continued. Because Raya and I were so skinny, the orderlies would place both of us on the same stretcher and carry us to the hospital basement during bombings. It was pitch-black down there, and only when the exploding bombs lit up the cellar could we see how crowded it was.

During one such night, there was a sudden commotion. I heard some men speaking Russian as they tried to calm down an unruly comrade. "Misha," a voice entreated, "we'll make you a cup of hot tea; just be patient a little longer." When another bomb exploded, I glimpsed the face of a madman. The look in his eyes clearly revealed that he was not in his right mind. I fervently hoped we could soon go back to our quiet room to get away from Misha. He frightened me.

After the raid was over, we were carried back to our room. No sooner did I fall asleep than I was awakened by the sound of our door being opened. In crept Misha. He didn't speak, and his movements were stealthy like those of a cat stalking its prey. And then he saw me. Because Raya was facing the window and I the door, he didn't see her, just me.

He padded over to my bed ever so quietly, bent over and put his face close to mine, and stared into my eyes. My heart pounded so hard that I thought my eardrums would burst. He then lay down on my bed at my feet and curled into a ball. I don't know how long he lay there, but it seemed like an eternity. At the sound of voices in the hall, Misha jumped up and hid behind the door. A nurse opened it and screamed when she saw Misha hiding there. Two men dressed in white rushed in with ropes and tried to subdue Misha. He fought back ferociously, but was overpowered. I felt sorry for him, as he looked so pitiful all tied up.

I am grateful he did not harm me, but the incident traumatized me. To this day I sometimes wake up in the middle of the night, my body tense and heart pounding, feeling a presence next to my bed.

Raya and I recovered and returned to the camp, and life went on as before. While the grown-ups continued to work at the factories, a woman who had attempted to supervise us at the old camp now managed to teach us how to read the clock. That would be the only education I would receive for quite some time. When she was not teaching us, we children pelted one another with sticks and stones. However, we were a close-knit group that looked out for one another, and we did not cause serious injuries despite our roughhousing.

I slept on the top bunk, as I had previously, but the mattress was not as comfortable as the one in the hospital. It felt as if it were filled with straw, because sharp things kept poking me. In addition, lice were constantly chewing on my scalp. And if that wasn't bad enough, the bedbugs crawling on the ceiling kept dropping onto my face. Because they feed on human blood, my face would be streaked with blood each morning when I awoke—I had squashed them on my cheeks in my sleep.

The neighbors in the room on the other side of ours were a couple, the Shtepas, who shared their room with a man whom I called Uncle Vanya. Both Raya and I called the couple Grandma and Grandpa, more out of respect than because of their age, since they weren't that old. Grandma Shtepa was a broad-shouldered woman and rather muscular-looking. She had a round, smiling face and wore her hair in long braids that she wrapped around her head. Most of our women wore their hair in braids. Her husband was a tall, handsome man with wavy brown hair and a handlebar mustache. His eyes always twinkled as if he were up to some mischief, and when he smiled, which was often, his mouth seemed to light up, since several of his front teeth were made of gold.

Raya and I loved being with Grandpa Shtepa. He looked like a cavalry man from a long time ago, and we envisioned him riding a white stallion and rescuing a princess. We thought it a special treat when he placed us on his knees and told us fairy tales.

Like me, Raya lacked a male role model in her life. I never knew what happened to her father, but her mother had been a circus performer in her younger years and was an attractive lady. After the war was over, a very nice man befriended her and took all of them under his wing.

Raya and I rejoiced when Grandpa Shtepa and all the grown-ups returned to the camp from the factory each day. The two of us would snuggle up to Grandpa and beg him to tell us more of his fairy tales. One of our favorites was the famous tale called "Johnny the Little Fool."

Johnny, the son of poor parents, was not bright, and was considered the laughingstock of the village. An evil, seven-headed dragon kidnapped the czar's daughter, and the czar offered half his kingdom and his daughter's hand in marriage to whoever rescued her. Johnny prepared himself to go and rescue the princess. All the villagers laughed at him, and his parents begged him not to go, but Johnny was determined to fight the evil dragon that spewed fire from all seven heads. As Johnny entered the city on his mule, he was met by a retinue of valiant, handsome young men who had the same noble intentions as Johnny.

According to Grandpa Shtepa, Johnny fought the dragon, using his wits more than his might. Of course he defeated the dragon, and the czar gave him his daughter and half of his kingdom. The czar figured that anyone who could perform such a feat was good enough for his daughter. They lived happily ever after, and no one laughed anymore at Johnny, the Little Fool, for he was now a prince.

"Oh, Grandpa, please tell us another story!" Raya and I would beg.

"Now, now, girls," he inevitably replied. "Go to your rooms and sleep, for we know not if the raids might come tonight. If all goes well, we'll continue tomorrow." As I lay in bed at night, I would imagine the beautiful palace and the princess, and I'm sure Raya did the same.

The Shtepas, kind as they were, were also hurting. They were separated from their teenage son, who had been taken by the Nazis to dig ditches and work in factories. According to the Shtepas, he was a tall, handsome young man, and their hearts ached because they didn't know whether he was dead or alive.

The Shtepas immigrated to America after the war and settled in Rochester, New York. Years later, during Gorbachev's reconstruction, the Shtepas found their son, who came to America and visited them for several weeks. How happy they were for this long-awaited reunion! He had a family back home in the Ukraine, and was educated, and they were very proud of him. The Shtepas led a life of peace and happiness until their deaths.

The Shtepas' roommate in the camp, the man I called Uncle Vanya, took an interest in Mother. He was a tall, handsome, intelligent man with a degree in electrical engineering. The war had separated him from his wife and daughter, who were back home in the Ukraine. However, Mother had no romantic inclinations, as she was still married to and in love with Father. She considered Uncle Vanya a friend, which he tried to be.

We heard from Father only twice after he was taken away. He sent us postcards in which he begged for his boots and pants. Unfortunately, they had been destroyed when our room was bombed in the first camp, but Mother's compassionate coworkers at the factory pooled their money and she was able to send him boots and pants, along with stale bread and tobacco.

As time went on and we didn't receive any more postcards from Father, Uncle Vanya encouraged Mother to go to Nero and ask how she could obtain information on my father's status. Mean as he was, Nero seemed to have some respect for my mother. She was pretty and didn't need a translator, since she spoke German fairly well. I think this may have flattered his nationalistic pride. He gave her the address in the city to which she needed to go to obtain the information she wanted, along with a permission slip to leave the camp. When she finally found the office, the authorities there cursed at her in German and refused to help her. Undaunted, she did not give up. She explained that she was still young and might want to remarry, but could not unless she knew whether her husband was dead or alive.

Sometime later Nero handed her an envelope containing Father's death certificate. It claimed that he died of "inflammation of lymph nodes" on October 3, 1944, in Buchenwald concentration camp. Mother broke down and sobbed. The Shtepas and Uncle Vanya tried to comfort her; she was a widow at the age of 26 and had a young child. I was heartbroken because I would never see my father again.

As we got hungrier, people began to get sick and die. We watched as corpses were carried out on stretchers and loaded onto trucks to be driven away. In an effort to keep the prisoners alive for factory work, Nero allowed us to go out on Sundays to neighboring villages to beg for food, a privilege that had been previously curbed at the opening of the new camp. He knew we would come back. There was no place for us to run and hide.

One windy autumn Sunday, Mother wrapped herself in her tattered army blanket, took me by the hand, and started walking down the country road toward a village to beg. As we walked we saw a blond, one-armed man in an orchard breaking dry branches off the trees. Apples, glorious apples, littered the ground. Shy, ill-dressed, skinny, and dirty, Mother continued walking past. Back home in Ukraine, our own orchards had been much larger and more lush than this one, and it pained her to realize she was reduced to begging from someone with much less than we had once had. All of a sudden a voice inside her head told her to turn back and ask the man for some apples.

"*Herr*, can you please give us some apples?" asked Mother. "The ones on the ground?"

The fair-haired man looked at us and smiled. "Why don't you come in and meet my family?" he replied in a friendly tone, pointing to a little white house with a large garden surrounded by the orchard.

The kitchen was bright and clean, and a pleasant, round-faced German woman wearing a white apron and three young girls sat at the table ready to have lunch. We were overwhelmed by the aroma of food. We learned that the father had lost his arm on the Eastern Front. Mother shared that Father had died in Buchenwald. In silence we ate simply but in plenty.

While the grown-ups visited after the meal, the youngest daughter, who was my age, invited me to play in the attic. Not sure if I understood German, she took me by my hand and gently pulled me as I followed her. "Come to our attic. We have a swing that you can swing on." She also had several toys that I had never seen before: handmade doll furniture with bedding, doll clothes, and the little swing that hung from the rafters. What struck me was how kind she was to me, a complete stranger from a labor camp.

As we left we were laden with food and hand-me-down clothing for me. "Please," they said, "return when you can." And we did. As it became colder, the oldest daughter, an accomplished seamstress who worked in a military uniform factory, fashioned a coat for Mother to replace her old army blanket and made a woolen cap for my lice-infested head.

Throughout the winter and into spring this family saved us from starvation. They themselves had very little, but, oh, how rich they were in spirit!

By the spring of 1945 the bombings from the Allies increased with such frequency and intensity that they no longer occurred only during the night, but throughout the day as well. The adults were unable to go to work at the factories under such heavy fire, so we all spent our time sitting in the foxholes and ditches within the camp. We didn't have a bomb shelter, as we had had at the old camp, so when we moved into the new camp, the men and women had been given pickaxes and shovels to dig holes to which we could run for cover during bombardments.

As we sat in those ditches, we watched silver planes glitter against the blue sky as they reflected the sunlight. Some exploded and went down in a fiery stream of smoke. We felt awful knowing that good men were dying in an effort to save us. We spent so many hours sitting in those ditches; the men playing cards and telling off-color jokes to pass the time and ease the tension while the women and children huddled together in fear.

I vividly remember our last night as prisoners in that camp. We kept wandering in and around the camp, looking for places to hide from the unceasing rain of bombs and bullets. At this point the guards had disappeared in an attempt to save their own lives.

A large group of us had found a bunker outside the camp to hide in that had a huge lid covering the entrance. We were all lying facedown, stacked up on top of one another like pancakes. I lay on top of a man who kept commenting, "How pleasant it is to the ear to hear the whistle of bullets flying over our heads." Meanwhile Mother, who was lying on top of me, would scream at the man, but actually in my ear, "You coward! What are you doing here among us women and children? Get out and go fight like a man!" The situation would have been comical if it had not been so serious.

Finally the night began to grow quiet. The lid to our hiding place opened, and a French prisoner of war said to us in broken German, "Stay still a while longer. The Germans are losing the war, and the Americans are coming."

After a while it became completely silent. As a new day dawned we heard birds singing, and we finally opened the bunker lid. The sunshine hurt our eyes as we climbed out of our hiding place because we had been in darkness for so long. When our eyes adjusted to the light, we saw the Americans far off on the hill making their way toward us, their tanks and trucks emblazoned with the white star.

We wanted to run to them but couldn't because the field that separated us was heavily littered with bodies and smoldering military vehicles. I was so emotionally numb at that point that the only thought I had was annoyance because those bodies held up our progress in reaching our deliverers.

But soon indescribable joy and happiness filled my heart. We were free, prisoners no more! I imagine it was much like what we will experience when Jesus returns to this earth to take us home to heaven. We were laughing and crying at the realization that we were also free from fear and hunger. There would be no more running, hiding, or persecution.

Never before had we seen smiling soldiers, but these Americans were so friendly. I could see compassion and pity in their faces as they looked at our skinny, undernourished, dirty bodies dressed in torn, filthy clothes.

The first thing they did was build fires, hang kettles, and cook oatmeal for us. What a shock. In our culture oats were for horses, not for human consumption! But it tasted so good. To this day my husband and I have oatmeal nearly every morning, and we never tire of it.

After we ate our fill, we headed back to the camp, the only "home" we knew, to find out who had survived and who had not. As Mother and I walked along holding hands, we found ourselves on the crest of a hill overlooking the camp. All of a sudden she jerked my hand to get my attention and peered into my face. "Alla," she said, choking on tears, "the war is over!"

And I thought to myself, *Sleep, I want to sleep. No more hiding, no more hunger.* I needed rest badly.

"But your father is dead," she continued, and I saw the anguish in her eyes.

Suddenly I was angry with Father, and my heart wrung with pain. Why did he have to die? Why couldn't he just wait a little longer? Then all three of us could have been together again. The thoughts raged through my mind as though the circumstances had been within his control. Then the anger turned into pity for Father, Mother, and me. I comforted myself with the thought that we would go back home to the Ukraine, to our village, for surely we still had some family left there.

But this was not to be. God had other plans for our future.

From a distance we saw that our barracks were still intact and that the American soldiers were busily tearing down the fence with their tanks. I like to think the Americans took care not to bomb those buildings, knowing they were full of innocent prisoners.

As we came closer, I saw Raya sauntering toward us, and my heart leaped with joy. Raya was alive! I wanted to run and hug her, but she strutted with such haughtiness that my feelings were hurt.

"Hey, Alla," she crowed with pride. "Wanna know what we just did?"

"What?" I asked.

"We just killed Nero!" she replied smugly.

"How did you do that?" I gasped.

"Remember the pickaxes Nero gave us to dig the foxholes and ditches? Well, we used those to hack him to death."

We were both desensitized, hardened little 9-year-old girls. Raya relayed the story with great self-importance, which made me mad at my mother for not having walked faster. Then I too could claim to have killed Nero and feel as important as Raya did. I now know that God must have spared me from being there—I had experienced more than enough violence for my young age.

"After that we threw him into the river," Raya continued. "You should have seen him lying in there with just his boots sticking out of the water!" She grabbed her stomach with both hands and bent over, laughing hysterically. Still choked with mirth, she then explained how Nero's daughter came afterward and had his body taken away.

For the next several weeks I heard people continuing to brag, "Boy, did we fix that dog, Nero!" And I would think to myself, *He was only one man. How many people did it take to kill him?* Many years later I would find out.

But we still had to "take care of" that woman translator who had added so much to our misery. A few weeks later she was found and brought back to the camp to face a day of reckoning. How she had changed! She had lost

« Babushka Natasha, Grandpa Anton, Aunt Katya, and my favorite uncle, Bill (Slavyansk, Ukraine, 1945)

≽ Grandpa Gregory (Ukraine)

« Sitting on Mother's lap and Father wearing his railroad uniform. This is the only photo in which the three of us are together (Slavyansk, Ukraine, 1938).

» Grandma Barbara with her third husband and daughter, Alexa (Ukraine, 1967)

« Father and Mother. Here Mother is pregnant with me (Prokopivka, Ukraine, 1935).

« We reenacted the Nazis' loading us onto trains bound for Germany for this photo (Leipheim, Germany, 1948).

» A German forced labor camp just like ours (Leipheim)

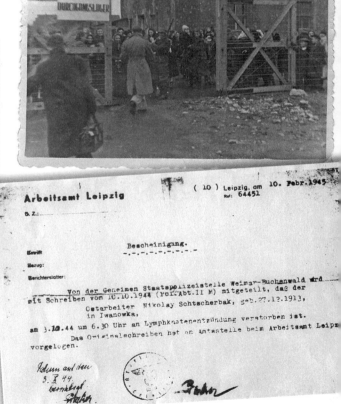

⌃ Soon after the Americans rescued us. I am wearing the dress made by the German church women and holding the doll Uncle Vanya gave me. Notice how big my shoes are! (Leipzig, Germany, 1945).

⌃ Father's death certificate from Buchenwald concentration camp. He died at the age of 30.

Sewing class at Somme Kaserne displaced persons' camp (Augsburg, Germany, 1945)

To the left of the adult, I was placed in the back because I had no uniform (Somme Kaserne).

Our scouts clubs. These are the buildings parents threatened to jump from if forced to go back to the Soviet Union. Also, my husband, Wesley, is one of the boys in this photo, but I didn't yet know of his existence until I came to America (Somme Kaserne).

Mother and Uncle Vanya on their wedding day (Somme Kaserne, 1948)

Reunited with my childhood friend Volodya, with his little brother, Alex, Jr. (Mittenwald, Germany, 1946)

⌃ I am in full traditional dress, expected of every Ukrainian girl (Somme Kaserne).

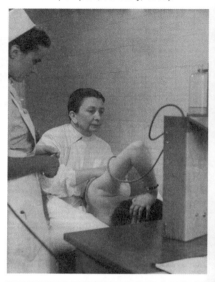

⌄ My first pneumothorax treatment performed by the kindly Jewish woman doctor (Kempten, Germany, 1950).

⌃ Sleeping outdoors, even in winter, was an important part of our treatment. I am second from the left (Kempten).

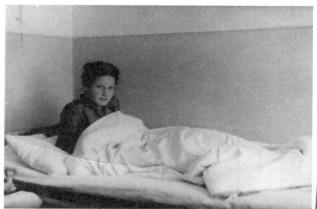

⌃ My first day in quarantine after being diagnosed with full-blown tuberculosis (Germany, 1950)

⟩⟩ Colorful robes the nurses made for us before leaving for Sweden; I am second from the left (Kempten, 1951).

« Celebrating Fasching, the annual costume carnival in Germany. I am second from the right, next to the German doctor who took such good care of us (Kempten, 1951).

⌄ Fellow travelers celebrating the journey to a new country (Sweden, 1951)

⌃ Finally released from the sanitarium and reunited with Mother in Spånga, Sweden (1952).

⌄ The beautiful sanitarium that welcomed us in Småland, Sweden (1951).

⌃ Exploring Stockholm, a common interest Uncle Vanya and I shared.

« My little brother, George, and I posing for the Swedish royal family photographer. This photo was published in a Stockholm newspaper, along with an article about Ukrainians celebrating Christmas (1955).

⋎ Mother (front left), with little George (front center) reunited with the most precious of friends, Alex, Jr., Uncle Alex, Aunt Lydia, and Volodya.

⋎ My dear Swedish friend Birgit (right) and I in front of the Swedish Royal Dramatic Theater. We still continue to stay in touch (Stockholm, 1960).

⌃ My first job. I was a secretary in Stockholm.

⌃ Newly arrived in America, I am waiting for my first date with Wesley (Brooklyn, New York, 1960).

My handsome Wesley with his parents (Manhattan, » New York). Wesley was in the military during the Korean War.

Our Greek Orthodox wedding took place on November 20, 1960, in Manhattan, New York.

⌃ With our first precious child, Victor (Brooklyn, 1961)

《 Wesley and I going to a New Year's ball (Brooklyn)

⌃ Our young family in Peekskill, New York

Mother (right) reunited with Grandma and Grandpa Shtepa from the forced labor camp (Rochester, 1962)

⌃ On the joyous occasion of my baptism, the children are with me as I am presented with my baptismal certificate (Peekskill, 1973).

« Mother (right) celebrating her American citizenship with Mayor George Pataki (center), who later became governor of the state of New York (Peekskill)

≽ My emotional reunion with Aunt Katya, Father's sister (right), whom I hadn't seen in 52 years (John F. Kennedy Airport, New York, 1993)

≽ Sharing my story with a classroom of precious students (Chattanooga, Tennessee)

≽ Wesley and I today, with our three children and their spouses, and five grandchildren. Oh, how richly blessed I am! (Chattanooga, 2012). Front row (left to right): daughter-in-law Stefanie and granddaughter Emily; Alla; husband, Wesley; and granddaughter Shelby. Back row: son Jerry, grandson Nikolaus, grandson Conner, son Victor, daughter-in-law Rene, grandson Alex, son-in-law Jim, and daughter Natalie.

weight, appeared older and scared, and was no longer as confident and imposing as she had been only a short time before.

I recall one of the American soldiers climbing into an open jeep and sitting next to her. We, the former prisoners, who had now turned into a mob, formed two rows on each side of the jeep, leaving just enough space for the jeep to squeeze through between us. We armed ourselves with stones, and I am ashamed to admit I was among the crowd along with my young friends. Even we children had caught the spirit of hatred and revenge.

But then something happened that enraged and shamed us all at once. After driving only a few feet, the driver stopped, took off his steel helmet, and placed it upon his passenger's head. She looked pitiful and comical at the same time. As they continued to drive away slowly, I could see her face clearly, but the helmet was too large for her head and covered her eyes. It kept bobbing up and down, making her look like a giant mushroom. Not a muscle moved in her petrified face. We understood the soldier's gesture, though. It was as if God Himself were saying: "That's enough, people! The war is over; you had your revenge when you killed Nero. Now leave this poor woman alone."

This simple gesture spoke to us all and showed us that while the soldier was a gentleman and possibly a Christian, we were behaving like a pack of hyenas. He tried to protect her because she was a defenseless woman. We, not wanting to injure him because he was our liberator, dropped our rocks and stones to the ground like the Pharisees in the Temple court of old.

There was yet another person to be found, although for reward and not punishment. With our help, the Americans were able to locate the well-liked guard who never abused us. He also looked thin and haggard, and we could see he was nervous. He did not know what fate awaited him, so he was surprised when our men put him on their shoulders and marched through the camp, cheering and laughing. After they set him down, we loaded him with food, and the Americans, seeing how we treated him, sent him on his way, free.

We continued living at the camp for a few more months, waiting as the Allied powers met and divided Germany into four sectors: American, British, French, and Russian. Meanwhile, refugees whom we had never seen before began arriving in our camp.

One day as Mother and I strolled aimlessly around the camp square, we saw in the distance a man walking toward us. He was skinny and shabbily dressed; his shoulders were slumped and his head shaved. As we came closer, I noticed his head was covered with scars and deep welts from beatings. We could see he was young, but very aged at the same time. Suddenly he stopped, and an almost grotesque grin appeared on his face. Mother gasped. It was Boris, Tina's husband.

"Dusia," began Boris, "where is Tina? Do you know anything about her and our daughter?"

Mother, with a trembling voice, described in detail what occurred that fateful night when the bomb struck our corner room.

He didn't cry. He had run out of tears. But the pain he felt in his heart was written on his face.

Now it was Mother's turn to ask about my father. She told him about the death certificate she had received from Buchenwald, stating that he had died of inflammation of the lymph nodes. He looked at my mother with a smile of pity. "No," he said, "don't believe those murderers. I was there with him. I saw it all. We worked in a quarry and had to cart heavy loads of rock. But your Nikolai was too weak, and he kept tripping and falling, causing his wheelbarrow to tip and dump all the rocks out. The guard became aggravated, called one of the German shepherds, and ordered it to tear out Nikolai's throat. He bled to death."

How my poor Mother sobbed, and my heart ached for her. I know only God could have given her the strength to go on with her life as she did, to enjoy it and be an encouragement to others.

"Besides," continued Boris, "your Nikolai was a fool. If only he had taken bread from the weaker ones, he would have survived. But, no, he wouldn't."

As we parted, Mother whispered to me, "Apparently that's how Boris survived—taking bread from the others." He was the only one of that group who came back, and we never saw him again.

* * *

The American tanks continued to thunder through the camp, tearing down the barbed-wire fence. American soldiers mingled with us and gave us lots to eat. There was no more hunger, no more fear, and the future seemed bright.

But even with all these good things in life, bad things continued. There was almost no law or order, and in our elation, we, the ex-prisoners, wanted revenge. Because the Americans wanted to pacify us, they allowed us three days to pillage the neighboring villages and the German civilians. I observed that human passion and greed knew no bounds. Our people took watches, bicycles, musical instruments, tools, china, bedding, and, of course, any alcohol they could get their hands on, which caused drunkenness and added even more violence among us. While intoxicated, one young man shot and killed his friend for no good reason. There was no punishment, but the young man cried bitterly as we buried his friend. Such a waste of a precious life. And as if there wasn't enough devastation and chaos, I know we took from many of the same Germans who had shared their food with us and risked their lives to help us while we were imprisoned.

I recall standing close to the road that passed by our camp while three of our men were standing in the middle of it talking and laughing. Their arms were folded across their chests, and I could see three or four wristwatches on each of their arms. There they stood, seeming quite pleased with themselves for having taken them from the Germans.

At that moment a German girl came by riding on a bicycle. She must have been about 17 years old and was very pretty. Her brown braids dangled in the wind, and her cheeks were rosy. She wore a typical German dress: a white blouse with short puffy sleeves, a flower-printed jumper, and a little white apron that was worn more for looks than practical use. The Germans called that dress *Dirndl*. When our men saw her coming, they blocked her way and ordered her to get off the bike. I saw the fear and hurt written all over her face. Her eyes were filled with tears, and her lips trembled. Obediently she got off her bike and handed it over. I felt sorry for the girl, but then again, I thought, *She's lucky they let her go.* There were bushes lining the side of the road where they could have taken her. I never forgot that ugly sight.

We former prisoners were certainly transformed in appearance. Now our women wore beautiful dresses and gold earrings, necklaces, bracelets, and rings. And yet, despite the unfairness of it all, a small group of German church members came to befriend us. I remember that two of the women took me to their home and sewed a dress for me within a matter of hours.

Mother and I did not forget the German family who had helped us throughout the winter. We continued to visit them, but now to give them food. They were the ones suffering now, while we had plenty to share. Because Mother was such a practical, courageous person, she invited the family to the camp and led them straight to the food distribution location. "Officer," Mother addressed the American in charge, "these people fed us while we were starving. Please give them some food."

The man was friendly and said, "OK, no problem. Take whatever you can carry."

Even Max, the man who used to bring me "pink pudding," showed up, and Mother and I went to his apartment for a friendly visit. I found it very exciting to take a street car through the city of Leipzig. We would later find out how providential that ride was.

* * *

One day a couple showed up at our camp. On closer inspection, I recognized little Nicky's mother and her well-built young boyfriend. He didn't look like a bad guy, but looks can be deceiving. She recognized me and smiled, but I could tell it was forced. She was wearing on her head a typical Russian scarf: bright yellow with red roses and green leaves, and gold thread woven throughout. In my culture a scarf like that would be considered a very special gift, and I figured that her boyfriend probably gave it to her. But how she could live with her conscience, I did not know.

Meanwhile, Uncle Vanya, the man who had lived in the room next to us in the barrack, was competing with two other suitors who were vying for Mother's attention. He gave me a beautiful doll, no doubt taken from some little German girl in an effort to win my mother's and my affections. He was jealous of a Frenchman who had taken an interest in Mother and who gave me honey cakes sent from his family back home. I remember thinking the Frenchman had eyes only for me when he smiled and presented the wrapped package to me while a group of us were sitting on a blanket having a picnic. But when he joined us and cozied up next to Mother, I immediately understood that I was just a means for him to get to my mother. But I didn't mind as long as I benefited from his pursuit.

There was also an American soldier interested in Mother who had more serious intentions. Johnny, from New Jersey, begged Mother to wait for him while he went back home to sponsor Mother and me to come to America. He promised to marry Mother and give me a good education. I liked him best of all. He was a gentle soul, very playful, thoughtful, and generous. He gave Mother dollars, and he reminded me very much of my father. I remember he used to bring us his helmet full of fresh farm eggs, but since we had no way to cook them, Raya, her brothers, and I would pierce each end of the eggs with a nail and suck out the insides. The egg whites tasted watery, but the yolks were smooth and creamy, and we enjoyed them.

Mother suspected that Johnny was younger than she and therefore was not interested in him. Later she explained to me that she was looking for a man and not a boy.

Chapter **20**

The time finally came when the division of Germany was complete, and we found ourselves and our old camp assigned as part of the designated Russian sector. So as the Americans began to slowly withdraw, the Soviets began to move into our camp.

Some of the French were still around, however, and frequented our camp because they liked our girls. The girls thought them charming, and this provoked our Ukrainian young men to jealousy. So much so that they began misbehaving by yanking the girls' hair or tripping them as they passed by. The naive young women complained to the Soviet authorities—a big mistake. "You traitors!" they shouted at the girls. "Why don't you stick to your own kind? Have nothing to do with foreigners!" Emboldened, our young men chased and caught some of the girls and shaved off their hair.

Alcohol continued to flow freely in our camp. Drunkenness, fighting, and shootings became commonplace. One day during such mayhem, a Soviet soldier yelled at us, "You, traitors, wait until you get back home. The 'Mother Hen' will find out who her chicks are. *Batushka* [Daddy] Stalin will take care of you!" We knew we were being threatened for having ended up in Germany. All we wanted was to go back to our homelands, but now we were afraid and began to have second thoughts.

During this time of transition, while the Americans continued to withdraw from our area and the Soviet authorities were taking over the reins, we patiently waited as the Soviets worked on a plan to load us onto trains and take us back home.

I would later hear rumors that many survivors from the Russian sector did not make it home for as many as 10 years. They were interrogated and imprisoned for their "cooperation" with the Germans during the war. This most likely would have been Mother's and my fate, but God in His infinite mercy had other plans for us, and our lives changed in a single, pivotal moment.

The new man officially in Mother's life, the man I called Uncle Vanya, had collected a number of watches and cameras during the time of pillaging the locals and had also taken a very valuable radio, which must have belonged to a military "higher-up." It was very powerful and could pick up news from the BBC and from other nations. A knowledgeable and intelligent man, he knew its worth and usefulness in terms of world communication and political news outside our sphere.

One day two Soviet officers drove up to our barrack on motorcycles while Uncle Vanya, Mother, and I stood outside talking, a family for all appearances.

One of the officers got off his motorcycle, strode up to Uncle Vanya, and pointed his finger at him. "You!" he said authoritatively. "You've got that radio. Hand it over to me now!"

I watched Uncle Vanya go pale. He had made the mistake of bragging about his possession, and there were no secrets in the camp.

"Wait, I'll go and pack it for you," said Uncle Vanya. After a few minutes, he brought out a heavy package wrapped tightly in burlap.

"Put it in the sidecar," ordered the officer. Uncle Vanya obeyed.

No sooner did the officers leave, the cloud of dust from the motorcycles still filling the air, when Uncle Vanya, pale and hands shaking, turned to Mother and said, "Dusia, let's run! I wrapped several bricks in that burlap. The radio is still in my room. When they find out, they'll come back and shoot all three of us!"

Now it was Mother's turn to be frightened. She immediately turned to me and quietly and carefully gave me instructions. "Alla, walk slowly out of the camp, go to the streetcar stop—the one we went to when we visited Max—and wait for me."

My heart beating rapidly, I did as I was told. We knew we were always watched by the Soviets in our camp and did not want to be seen leaving together. The streetcar stop was a long walk away for a lone, scared 9-year-old. As I stood waiting, many strangers passed me by, some carrying bundles on their shoulders, but all trying to catch a ride. The American soldiers, shaved, smiling, and dressed in their spiffy uniforms, were easy to spot in the crowd. Everyone else was shabbily dressed and wore worried expressions on their faces. But no one paid attention to me, for which I was glad. As I waited, many troubling thoughts raced through my mind. *Will Mother come? What if the bad man discovered the bricks and came back before she could leave? What if they arrested her and Uncle Vanya?* My father was dead and Babushka Natasha far away. *What would happen to me?* And then I saw Mother coming! How relieved I was when she finally arrived.

Shortly afterward Uncle Vanya arrived as well with watches on his arms, cameras dangling around his neck, and that silly radio that still could cost us our lives. He would keep that radio almost until the day he died.

We boarded the next streetcar and rode to Max's apartment, looking for shelter. Max was gracious and let us stay the night, and in the morning we found a coal train heading south to the American sector in Bavaria. Since we had already experienced American kindness, we thought we could find safety with them. We had only a few dollars and needed to save them for food, so we climbed up and sat on top of the pile of coal. We found other refugees like us, as well.

When the train stopped at a station, we observed many Slavic people traveling north, trying to get back to their home countries. During one such stop, we watched these returning people pull out an accordion and start dancing and singing. We were later told that most of them ended up in Siberian prisons.

One of the Slavic men saw a woman standing next to me on the coal car and yelled, "Auntie, do you speak Russian?" She wouldn't answer and pretended not to understand. Then he turned to me, "Hey, you, little girl, do you speak Russian?" My heart beating wildly, I too pretended not to understand. If I had replied, they would have dragged us off the train and accused us of being traitors for not traveling north with them, which would take us back home. They would realize we were heading south for the American sector, proof we were running away from home. Another close call! I know without a doubt angels were still watching over us.

Without further incident, we finally made it to the city of Augsburg. After Mother, Uncle Vanya, and I climbed down from the coal car, we needed to find a place to stay the night. No friends or relatives came to greet us—we were on our own. The city had been bombarded like so many other cities, so we decided to search for a place among the abandoned ruins, which were not difficult to find. We found a three-story stone house at the end of a block located near the center of the city. It had been partially blown up and was completely empty, except for rats and mice. We chose a corner room on the first floor with a blown-out window, but at least we had a roof over our heads. We slept, half lying and half sitting, on the cement floor, which was littered with rocks and debris. As night approached and we began to be overcome by slumber, we could feel rats scampering over our legs.

Uncle Vanya and Mother wasted no time. The next morning they went to look for food to buy and also for places where other refugees stayed.

It would be a couple of days before they found an abandoned school where hundreds of people like us were living. But as they went out in the mornings, they left me alone, instructing me to stay out of sight and not to leave our hiding place. But the sun was shining, and I became bored sitting in that debris-filled room with nothing to do. All I had to do was climb out through the window and step into the sunshine, which I did. That's when the German boys saw me, much to their delight. They armed themselves with rocks and stones, and I became their target. There were about three of them in their early teens. They knew I was a refugee and decided to give me a good scare. I jumped back through the window and huddled in the corner while the rocks flew through the open window and bounced off the wall. I heard them laughing and chattering in German. Just then Uncle Vanya and Mother came back, and my attackers fled. Mother found me sitting in the corner, scared and shaken. She did not reprimand me for disobeying her. Instead, she smiled and told me we were leaving right then.

We went to that abandoned school where we were offered floor space, blankets, pillows, and food. We hung woolen army blankets on nails so that men and women could dress in privacy. We were finally with people who were like us—Slavic refugees and former prisoners of war—who wanted to stay with the Americans.

Because there were more and more refugees flooding the city, the American authorities placed us in a larger facility, a former German military camp called Somme Kaserne. There were approximately 5,000 of us, and, again, we were overcrowded. We ended up sleeping in an attic that had been divided into small rooms. We slept on bunk beds and shared our tiny room with another unmarried couple. Even horse stables were divided into rooms and used as living quarters. But we were happy in our newfound security.

The main kitchen served food, and we stood in line with our tin cans and spent time getting acquainted and sharing our war experiences and backgrounds with one another. There were many professionals among us, such as teachers, artists, writers, engineers, doctors, professors, and priests, as well as seamstresses, shoemakers, and tailors.

The grown-ups realized that our education had suffered because of the war, so they organized a school of sorts, and we children had classes six days a week. To my great delight, we also formed our own churches, one for the Greek Orthodox and another for Catholics. I was 10 and started the first grade. But thanks to Uncle Vanya, who had already been tutoring me,

I was advanced enough to skip to the second grade, which made me happy.

But our peace and joy was short-lived. Rumor had it that Stalin claimed us as his citizens and demanded that President Truman return us to Soviet-held countries. This action included Russians, Ukrainians, Poles, and White Russians, as well as those from the Baltic countries, such as Estonia, Latvia, Lithuania, and so on. General Eisenhower, under pressure from President Truman, gave orders that the Americans assist the Soviets with this deportation.

We made a statement of defiance and mourning by putting black flags on top of the buildings in our camp. Committees representing the different ethnic groups in our camp began organizing themselves and joined with one another in a unified effort to appeal to the American authorities for aid in this matter. The Catholics, being the most organized, were a major force in our camp and headed up this campaign. We even threatened to organize a hunger strike.

In a matter of days the Americans gathered us into the main hall so we could listen to an address from a Soviet official. The man seemed very friendly, promised us a safe trip home, reunions with our families, and a good life, since the war was over. We knew better and didn't believe a word he said. Distrust ran deep—we had already experienced the Communistic regime once before. We started booing and swearing at the man as he left the stage, and as he made his way to his waiting car, I saw grown women sticking their tongues out at him. I thought they looked childish and silly.

As we exited the hall, we were shocked to find ourselves surrounded by both Soviet and American soldiers waiting to forcefully take us away in empty American military vehicles. Because we had had enough bloodshed, suffering, and pain, our adults decided if we were going to be placed in labor camps again, or sent to Siberia and probably shot, we should just end it here and now.

Somme Kaserne buildings were tall, and many families ran up to the fourth-floor attics, threatening to throw their children down first and then to jump out the windows themselves. Wishing us no harm, the Americans panicked and sent the Soviets away, removed the vehicles, and begged us to calm down. "There may be a way out of this," the Americans told us. "Let's go to the higher authorities on the other side of the city where our headquarters are located and discuss the situation. We will protect you." We agreed to their proposal.

As always, we turned to a higher power in a grave situation such as this. We had our priests, our spiritual leaders, and the next day they organized the 5,000 of us in a march through the city of Augsburg to the American headquarters.

The situation reminded me of my village back home when we had prayed for rain. Then we carried banners embroidered with silk and gold and depicting Jesus and the virgin Mary. But this time the priests were dressed in black, a sign of mourning. The choir sang mournful hymns, and the rest of us followed again: first the children, then the elderly, and then our parents behind us all. Traffic stopped as we made our way to the meeting place.

I vividly remember the sea of people at the American headquarters. At a table centered in the midst of the throng stood a high-ranking American officer dressed in military uniform, but with no tie. He looked kind of casual and was, of all things, chewing gum! We were shocked that a man of his rank would chew gum. To us he looked very undignified. There were two older women standing in front of me. One said to the other, "Look at him! He reminds me of a cow chewing its cud. And he's holding our lives in his hands?"

The man at the table asked the interpreter, "What do these people want?"

"They don't want to go back to their countries," replied the interpreter.

"That's fine. They can stay here. It's a democracy."

We forgave him his gum chewing! We were ready to kiss not only his hands, but his feet as well. In that moment we learned the wonderful meaning of democracy. Previously, we were always told what to do, or forced to do what we didn't want to do, but now we had the freedom of choice. We didn't walk back to the camp, but ran back laughing, hugging one another, and crying with joy.

We were advised, though, not to leave the camp late at night or venture out alone. The Soviets were kidnapping our people, especially the men, and the Americans could not guarantee our safety beyond the camp's grounds.

We later found out that other camps such as ours did not fare as well. During a time when life was quieter and safer, we refugees from all the surrounding camps visited one another, trying to find loved ones or get information leading to their whereabouts. It was during these visits we learned the horrors of how the Soviets forcefully seized our people from other refugee camps. Somehow our camp went unscathed, but in the other camps Soviet soldiers broke into the rooms, grabbed the men, and dragged them into waiting empty vehicles to be taken back home. Many men who weren't grabbed quickly enough ran to the windows and jumped to their deaths. Others cut their wrists or stabbed themselves in the stomach. The luckier ones ran out to hide in the fields and forests.

The Americans, who had the unenviable task of retrieving the bodies after these events, found the whole situation revolting. The war was officially over, treaties had been signed, and yet human suffering continued. To prevent these types of tragedies from continuing, I believe the Americans must have insisted that the Soviets approach our camp a little less aggressively when it came our turn to be taken away.

Approximately 8 million people found themselves outside their homelands by the end of World War II, most having been removed by the Nazis to work in slave labor camps. But the United Nations Relief and Rehabilitation Administration (UNRRA) had stepped in, and by December 1945 large numbers were repatriated. By the summer of 1947 less than a million of us remained, mostly eastern Europeans who did not wish to return to areas under Soviet control.

Now that we were less crowded, we organized ourselves even better. We established Scout-type clubs for the youth, choirs, theater and drama, and folk dance groups. The women organized arts and craft workshops and taught embroidery, a skill that no Ukrainian girl could do without. Religion was taught by a kind, elderly Greek Orthodox priest, whom we children dearly loved. He and his wife had previously suffered persecution for their faith, but they had stood firm, as had many of our clergy. The Catholics had their own instruction as well.

As for me, I was finally getting answers to my many questions about God. I found it a little disappointing to learn that He didn't live exclusively in my village church—I had wanted to keep Him for my own. But I was in awe to realize how mighty and great He was and how He cared for the entire world. I also believed that He heard and answered prayers.

Mother and Uncle Vanya continued living together, as many couples did. Under the circumstances, this was not considered unusual. Many families were broken up because of separation or death during the war. In time, most would marry legally, adopt one another's children, and have new ones.

Uncle Vanya wanted to marry Mother, but she was hesitant. He suffered from mood swings and slapped or punched her at the least provocation. He was belligerent and had an air of superiority; he constantly reminded her that she was just a farmer's daughter, while he was an engineer, even though she had a degree in chemistry and was also intelligent.

Meanwhile a man we knew who lived on our floor dropped by to say hello. He told us, "I visited the city of Mittenwald, where there are also displaced persons, and I met a lovely couple, Alex and Lydia."

Mother became excited. "Do they have sons?" she asked.

"Yes," the man replied. "They have two sons, Volodya and Alex junior."

"It's them!" cried Mother. It had been several years since she had last seen her dear friend and schoolmate.

Soon afterward, Mother and Uncle Vanya took a train and headed for Mittenwald, leaving me behind. While they were there, Mother opened up to Lydia and shared with her how Uncle Vanya wanted to marry her, but she still couldn't decide what to do. Mother was lonely and needed a man and stability in her life, but didn't feel confident that Uncle Vanya was the one to fill her needs.

"No problem," Lydia told her. "We have a clairvoyant here who calls up spirits. Maybe she can give you some advice." It was common among our people to hold séances to try to predict our futures. Mother and Lydia went to see the woman and sat down at a round table with saucers and letters of the alphabet spread out on the table.

"Whom do you want to call that you wish to speak to?" the woman asked.

"Call my father, Gregory, and ask him if I should marry Vanya," replied Mother.

Sure enough, a saucer began to move from letter to letter, spelling out a reply. "My child, do not disturb my peace."

Mother was shaken and decided to leave him alone.

Then the woman asked, "How about Rasputin?"

Now, Rasputin was the infamous monk who was said to have been able to stop the czar's hemophiliac son's bleeding. History tells us he was an immoral man who was able to influence the czar's wife to the extent that he was able to engineer political decisions and, in effect, ruin the czar's family and Russia. In the end, the Russian nobility threw him into a river, and he drowned.

Mother agreed to the suggestion and asked the same question: Should she marry Vanya? The reply was "If you marry him, you will be the greatest sinner in the world."

Mother was even more shaken and told Uncle Vanya about the visit with the clairvoyant and how she made the decision not to marry him.

He laughed and said, "Stop believing that nonsense and marry me anyway. I promise things will change once we get married." Over the course of many years to come, I would hear Mother mutter, "I should have listened to Rasputin!"

Despite their stormy relationship, Mother did fall in love, and the wedding day arrived. How well I remember that day. I was about 12 years old, and Mother had prepared a nice dinner in our tiny attic room. They didn't have an actual wedding ceremony—just the signing of some papers before a judge.

I realized I now had a stepfather who would never adopt me, but I couldn't understand why Mother married an abusive man. I was also angry at her because I still mourned the loss of my father and felt she was not faithful to his memory.

During the wedding dinner I just stood silently in defiant protest. Well, my attitude didn't go over well with my new stepfather. He would not tolerate such insolence from a pip-squeak such as I, and I would feel his wrath for many years to come. Mother ended up unhappy with the choice she had made and would regret it as well.

Sometime later the three of us went to Mittenwald, and I had the joy of seeing Aunt Lydia, Uncle Alex, and Volodya again, and, of course, meeting Alex, Jr. Everyone was happy and excited, yet Uncle Alex mourned the tragic death of his friend, my father. Later he would write a beautiful poem in Father's memory. I still have that poem today, and every time I read it I cry. They would later immigrate to Belgium, where Uncle Alex worked in the coal mines, but we continued to stay in touch.

Eventually both our families would settle and meet in America, and the friendship lasted until death began to part us. First, Volodya died of cancer at a young age, which broke Alex's and Lydia's hearts. But they found comfort in Alex, Jr., and his family. Later Uncle Alex died, and then my mother. When I called Aunt Lydia to tell her, we both cried bitterly. Our families had had so much in common and shared such a long history—all the suffering and persecution, but also the joy of becoming parents and grandparents. Less than a year later Aunt Lydia died. Only Alex, Jr., and I are still in this beautiful country, and we too stay in touch. He is happily married and has (as I do) two sons and a daughter and grandchildren. All are good productive citizens whose roots began long ago back home in the Ukraine with two teenage couples who were young and very much in love.

While we were still residents of Somme Kaserne, Mother kept busy and was very resourceful. She cleaned homes for the American officers' wives, and received payment in dollars, cigarettes, chocolate bars, and soap. She would pack these items into her backpack, hop on her rusty bicycle, and pedal to the nearest village. She would trade her wares and return with fruits, vegetables, chunks of ham, sausages, and cheese. We wanted the food, and the farmers wanted what she had to offer. She would sell some of the farm products to the people in our camp and make even more money. This enabled Mother to buy shoes and dresses for her and me and give Uncle Vanya money to buy film for his many cameras.

For all her effort, though, Uncle Vanya felt threatened by the success of Mother's thriving business, and there was great contention between them because of it. Once, Mother had opened the window and set her backpack out on the slanted roof of our attic room to air out, and Uncle Vanya, knowing it was there, left it in the rain. When Mother returned, he pulled it back through the window to show the dripping backpack to her and said, "See how stupid you are?" and slapped her face.

Uncle Vanya spent his time making sure the camp radio and loudspeaker system were in working order, and he always had a camera dangling from his neck. He loved to take pictures, even of me.

I, on the other hand, spent a lot of time fighting with the boys, as usual. I was skinny and tall for my age, my cheeks were hollow, which caused my nose to appear too large for my face, and I coughed a lot. The boys called me *Alka Palka* (Alla the stick). This clever rhyme was not a compliment. Provoked to anger, I would call them names also. One day a group of boys had had enough of me and decided to give me a good thrashing. But before they could catch me, I ran to the tall willow tree by my building and climbed up it. Halfway to the top I stopped long enough to spit at the boys down below, who were shaking their fists at me. Then they decided to follow me up while I continued my climb.

A man on the third floor who knew my parents saw me in the tree and yelled, "Shame on you, big girl, fighting with the boys! Don't you know how to behave any better?" By now the boys were closing in on me, so I grabbed several of the willow branches and slid back down to the ground and ran to safety.

As I entered our attic room out of breath, Mother and Uncle Vanya immediately began berating me for my behavior, already having learned from the man what I had done. I didn't mind. I was too pleased with myself for having outwitted the boys.

* * *

Uncle Vanya often complained to Mother in front of me, "If it weren't for *her*, our marriage would be happy." I felt guilty, and both Mother and I tried hard to please him. We even avoided provoking him to anger by keeping silent when he would eat most of the special food rations that were assigned to me after I was tested and found to be one of the weaker, sickly children.

But God sent me a special friend who gave me comfort. A young American soldier, about 19 or 20 at most, befriended me. It was not unusual for American soldiers to "adopt" us kids. I can't recall his name, but I do remember how awfully handsome he looked in his uniform, and he became my Prince Charming. He would come to the building we lived in and, with Mother's permission, take me for a walk in a park. Mother and I trusted him completely. He was friendly, gave me chewing gum and Uncle Vanya a pack of Camel cigarettes. We couldn't speak to one another—I knew no English and he knew no German—yet we did communicate through a sign language of sorts. We would point at things, nod, shake our heads, and smile.

He would always hold my hand as we walked through the park, which was a beautiful place with lots of trees and well-kept flower beds. We would play tag, and when he caught me, he would twirl me around in the air. He probably had a little sister back home and missed her. I also knew he must have been lonely, because he visited often with Mother, since she spoke some English.

But as the saying goes, all good things must come to an end. One day there was much excitement in our camp. The Americans were having a big dance party for their soldiers. My friends and I knew what that meant: lots and lots of cigarette butts to collect. We all noticed the American soldiers would draw only a few puffs on a cigarette and then throw it down on the ground.

We children would gather the butts up and give them to our men, who were too embarrassed to do so themselves. I would always give some of my butts to Uncle Vanya as a peace offering, but our men would reward us with pocket change. We spent that money at the circus and on carousel rides that were sometimes set up on the outskirts of Augsburg. So everyone profited.

We watched as instruments were carried into the giant dance hall, where tables were covered with white linens and flowers placed in the middle. Finally we saw soldiers and their dates entering the hall, the girls dressed beautifully and their escorts looking smart in their uniforms. When the orchestra played and the dancing was in full swing, we had our chance to dive under the tables and gather our "treasures."

It so happened that as I crawled from under one table to another, I accidentally bumped a man's well-polished shoe. Instantly the tablecloth was lifted up, and I stared, horrified, into my soldier friend's face. Initially we were both shocked. Next to him sat his date, smoking a cigarette. She was a very pretty girl and had auburn hair that flowed down her shoulders. I must admit I was jealous. She had an amused smile on her face when she saw me.

"Alla!" he almost shouted at me. "What are you doing here? Go home!"

Then he saw the half-smoked cigarette butts clutched in my hands and smiled. He let the tablecloth fall back into place, and I crawled my way back toward the exit, but not before I snatched a few more cigarette butts.

Surprisingly, he continued to come and take me to the park. But it was not the same. There were three of us now, and even though he still held my hand, *she* clung to his other arm. I didn't like her, the intruder; and I'm sure she didn't like me, the tagalong.

Summer was coming to a close, and one afternoon I was playing hide-and-seek outside with my friends. It was getting late and time for bed. When I dashed into our room, I could see that Mother's face was sad. "Alla," she began, "your friend came by to say goodbye."

My heart beat wildly. "Why?" I asked. "What happened?"

"His company has been transferred," she replied, "but he left you a gift."

She gave me a small package. It contained a bar of Lux soap, a chocolate bar, and one dollar. That was a lot of money to me. I put my treasures under my pillow and cried myself to sleep. I knew I would never see him again, but the sweet memories linger still.

Chapter **23**

any people continued to immigrate to other countries, such as England, Belgium, Brazil, Argentina, Australia, and Canada; and as our camp became too large for us, we were moved to a smaller camp away from the city of Augsburg, an area more rural and mountainous. The nearest village was Leipheim. We enjoyed our new surroundings, but more people continued to leave. We kept receiving letters from friends telling us how well they were doing, and we could hardly wait for our turn to be screened and allowed to travel to a new land that offered us jobs, a stable life, and a future.

Naturally everybody wanted to immigrate to the country that "flowed with milk and honey": America. Only the healthy were accepted, though, so applicants first had to go through a screening process. We, of course, applied to go to America as well.

Meanwhile, I signed up to attend a local German school. Even though we had previously studied some English and German, it was not enough, and I now wanted to become proficient.

Finally the day came for our turn to go to the health-screening camp for testing. We were all very nervous and excited. They X-rayed me several times, and there I stood, all skin and bones. I had full-blown tuberculosis.

The next day a special car quickly transported me far away to a children's hospital in Kempten, in southwestern Bavaria, because I was contagious. I had never cried so hard in my life as I did then. We had waited so long, and it was such a blow to our hopes and dreams. I was bitterly disappointed. All my girlfriends had been leaving for America, happy and excited, but I was left behind. I couldn't understand why it had to be me.

Mother and Uncle Vanya were crestfallen. If only we had known then the encouragement of Romans 8:28: "And we know that God causes everything to work together for the good of those who love God" (NLT). But we didn't.

I was 14 at the beginning of summer in 1950 when I arrived at the children's hospital. I was quarantined in a separate building and had a room to myself where the nurses delivered food and left quickly. The doctors didn't stay around too long either, just long enough to administer streptomycin injections into each of my legs. Many times the doctors would enter my room and find me on my knees praying. I had no one to talk to other than God. The doctors would always respectfully exit and return later.

I spent the entire summer alone with God and discovered that He was real, a friend, someone with whom I could actually have a relationship and talk to. During this time I would often ask, "Why me?" But I was neither bitter nor angry, just disappointed.

Because I required lots of rest and fresh air, two orderlies daily carried me outside on a stretcher and set me on a folding bed under a pear tree. The food was good, and I loved being there, but I was very lonely. Some girls my age would come from the main building and ask me my name and what country I was from. We were all of different nationalities, but we all spoke German. Of course they kept themselves at a safe distance, but I appreciated their company and kindness, for they, too, were sick.

It was during those hours under the pear tree that I would look up at the blue sky and watch birds hopping from branch to branch, singing happy songs, and wonder what was in store for my future. I was almost 15, and my education had been interrupted yet again.

By now Mother and Uncle Vanya were in Augsburg running a delicatessen store for the owner. They tried to visit occasionally, but it was difficult for them, since they didn't have a car.

The children's hospital had a laundry department where our bedding and clothes were washed. The man in charge was a nice person; he loved the kids, and they returned his affection. We considered him an old man— he was 53.

One day he came to visit me because he heard a new patient had arrived. He was Russian, a former soldier in the White Russian army who had fought for the czar. When the Czarist regime fell, he had fled to Bulgaria, and from there to Germany. He was not afraid of my germs and visited longer than anyone else. He had a large collection of wonderful books, most written in Russian. He shared them with me, and time went by fast. During my three months in quarantine, I was able to read many of the Russian classics by Chekhov, Tolstoy, Turgenev, and others. Some of these were inspired by true-life stories of people devoted to God, and I loved reading them. I was especially touched by Leo Tolstoy's *Resurrection*.

Finally, the time came when I was released from quarantine, but now the doctors needed to administer pneumothorax treatments to collapse my lung and speed up recovery. Shrinking the lung would also shrink the affected area, allowing the wound to calcify and heal. But surgery was needed first, as well as Mother's permission.

She arrived, very upset and concerned. It was then that she opened up to me and told me for the first time that she loved me. She explained that she had not been able to do so previously because my birth had caused her such trauma, and that when she had first looked at me the love never came. She had always taken care of and protected me, but I had always wondered why she never kissed or hugged me. My father had treated me more like a mother than she had. When she heard about the surgery, however, she was afraid I would die, and her long-hidden love awakened.

Mother signed the permission slip for my surgery, and I was transferred to another, more advanced hospital with my doctor at my side. The surgery freed the lung from the ribs and allowed air into the cavity so that the pneumothorax treatments could later be applied.

When I awoke from surgery, I saw a large cross hanging on the wall. I was hurting and perspiring heavily. Then two nuns dressed in black came and wiped my face with cool water. They were so compassionate and tenderhearted; their faces radiated goodness and love. After a few days in this hospital, I returned to the children's hospital and to my waiting friends. But now the treatments would begin.

I was taken to a small room where the doctor and nurse had me lie down on a table on my right side. The doctor pressed on the left side of my rib cage, looking for a spot to insert a needle. The needle was more like a thin nail because it was hollow with another thinner needle inside. As the needle punctured my pleural cavity, air was blown in around my lung, which compressed it so the affected area would shrink and heal. But sometimes they had a hard time finding an "empty pocket" between the ribs and the lung, so the doctor would keep reinserting the large needle into different areas until he found the right spot. I was considered a big girl and tried to be brave, but one day the doctor poked me 14 times, and I broke down and cried, really cried, from the tension and pain. In the beginning the treatments were done three times a week, and I felt as if I carried a brick in my chest; but soon they lessened to once a week, and in later years, once a month.

As the doctors gained more practice and my treatments lessened in frequency, it did become easier for me, and although the treatments would last for eight years, I led a fairly normal life.

Back at the children's hospital, I was housed in the main building and had a roommate, a girl from Latvia. She was 17, small, and sickly looking, with light brown hair, freckles, and blue eyes. I was her hands and feet, like a call nurse, bringing her water and anything else she needed. All this I did gladly, for she was worse off than I. She had tuberculosis of the spine and spent two years lying flat on her back in a giant cast. At that time, surgical knowledge was limited compared to what it is now. She spent her time either reading or knitting, but we liked one another and my lonely days were over.

The Americans paid tutors to teach us English, German, and math, and a woman taught us girls how to crochet and knit sweaters and shawls for ourselves and for the smaller children. We celebrated birthdays, which was special, and had a play at Christmas in which I was able to participate. Then in February the entire country celebrated an event called *Fasching*, a carnival, in which everyone dressed in costumes and attended parties, balls, and pubs. The next day the newspapers were splashed with pictures of celebrities and those who won awards for having the best costumes. After the war, this was a welcome diversion, and we children were lent costumes so that we could participate as well.

At the children's hospital there were only two doctors: a German man and a short, plump Jewish woman who wore her hair in a bun. She was very motherly, and we loved her. These two doctors, working harmoniously, were like parents to us, and with the extra-kind nurses, we children lived like one big happy family. We were all victims of war, different in nationality, but united in suffering and pain. We could see that the adults pitied us, having witnessed what the war had done to us innocent children, and they treated us exceptionally well.

We older children were encouraged to spend time with the little ones, who needed their mommies and daddies but instead were confined to their beds. We read to them, told them stories, or just sat by their beds to keep them company. My heart went out to them, and because of my lively imagination, I was a good storyteller. I also liked the spirit of camaraderie that existed among us all.

It had been about a year since I was first admitted to the children's hospital when several strikingly handsome strangers showed up at our hospital. They were tall, blue-eyed, well-dressed, and spoke an unusual language that none of us had ever heard before. We soon found out they were doctors and nurses from Sweden. They represented the Swedish Red Cross, and their country was extending an invitation to us and to our families. After a few weeks of physical examinations, testing, and paperwork, several of us who were willing to transfer to a hospital in Sweden were accepted.

But Uncle Vanya had other plans. He saw an opportunity to immigrate to America instead. "Dusia," he said gently. "Why not let Alla go to Sweden by herself, and when she gets well, she can join us in America?" For once Mother put her foot down. I was 15 years old, and she knew I needed her. Uncle Vanya was disappointed, having suffered yet another blow to his dreams, which added to their already strained relationship.

So Mother and Uncle Vanya accepted the opportunity and the promised jobs, and we were off to a different country again. We were given Swedish dictionaries and study materials, and I plunged wholeheartedly into learning the new language. By now I had studied German, English, Russian, and Ukrainian, which made it easier for me to learn yet another language.

We traveled slowly by train for several days, took a ferry in Denmark, and then crossed the channel to Sweden. I was driven to a sanitarium that was purposely located deep in the woods. In contrast to the children's hospital in Kempten, this building was a large beautiful mansion. It was well built and had tall ceilings, large rooms, an elegant dining room with chandeliers and a fireplace, and wide stairways with carved banisters.

I was joined there by two friends from the children's hospital in Kempten, along with additional patients like us from other parts of Germany. We, the newcomers from Germany, were treated like celebrities. In fact, the Swedish royal family's photographer came and took pictures of us to be put in the newspaper along with an article explaining who we were and why we had come to Sweden.

We loved the scent of the pine trees and slept on outside balconies, even if it snowed. We were bundled up and kept warm, the fresh air and rest vital to our rehabilitation along with nutritious food. Again, we were grateful for the high-quality care and treatment we received from the kind Swedish doctors and nurses.

Here I made new friends. My Swedish was limited, of course, but since I was not bashful, I used whatever I knew. The other foreign girls seemed to know so much more Swedish than I, but didn't practice it much because they were too shy and afraid of being ridiculed when they made mistakes. When I made mistakes, no one made fun of me. In fact, they helped me with my grammar and pronunciation, and I learned the new language well. That experience taught me that many things are possible and not to be afraid to try, especially since God had become the center of my life. I still continued to pray in the dark while kneeling beside my bed, despite the snickers I received from the other girls.

The sanitarium was for adults only, an exception having been made for us. On our floor was a young Russian woman, but she was separated from us in a room of her own. Her tuberculosis had progressed so far that she was dying. We were allowed to visit her only a few minutes each day. She was 25 years old, and her architect husband was 32. They were young, in love, and had a 5-year-old son. The whole situation was heartwrenching. She died and was placed in the sanitarium chapel, while we patients and the doctors and nurses surrounded her casket and mourned her lost youth. The grief-stricken husband stood there holding their son in his arms. She was a beautiful woman in life, and even in death she looked like a princess with her hair covering her shoulders and a peaceful look on her face. The only trace of life that remained was the wreath on her head that the nurses had fashioned from wildflowers, which grew in abundance in the woods. The occasion was a grim reminder to the rest of us how fragile life is.

Uncle Vanya felt it was not fair that Mother had me while he longed for a son of his own, so at age 35 she was expecting a baby. Upon our arrival in Sweden she had been placed in a Red Cross facility in the province of Småland, where she received prenatal care until the baby was born a few months later on December 16, 1951.

Meanwhile, Uncle Vanya traveled to Stockholm and stayed in a small house in the suburbs rented to us by the Salvation Army. He was also provided a job in a factory.

I was 16 when my new baby brother, George, arrived. What a bundle of joy! Mother was mature enough to enjoy her new baby, and her love for him knew no bounds. I, too, fell in love with him; he was the cutest thing I had ever seen. That winter when Mother and baby George left to join Uncle Vanya in Stockholm, I was permitted to go with them for a visit.

We traveled by train to be met at the station by Uncle Vanya and his new Ukrainian friend. Mother proudly presented their son. Uncle Vanya took one look, grimaced, and commented, "A piece of meat." Mother was deeply hurt by his response. But Uncle Vanya did love his son very much. Thinking back on Uncle Vanya's behavior over the years, I wonder if he simply had a chemical imbalance that needed treatment. Unfortunately, these things were not diagnosed or treated at that time.

After a week's visit, I had to return to the sanitarium. But by early summer I was well enough to be released, although I would have to continue the pneumothorax injection therapy for several years. After having spent a year in those beautiful surroundings and under the care of loving doctors and nurses, I thrived physically and emotionally and was ready to rejoin my family and start a new chapter in my life.

Uncle Vanya continued to work in the factory while Mother cleaned well-to-do people's homes. Babysitting my brother was the bright spot in my life. How I loved him! He was adorable, and I showered him with love and affection, feeling as if he were my own son. Today he is a grown man, happily married to a lovely wife, and has three bright children of his own.

There was a school in Stockholm that offered a GED program, so I applied to Swedish Social Services for assistance and was granted two years of education. But our education went beyond our textbooks. The principal of the school believed in enriched academics, so every Saturday, for at least three hours, he would show us slides of famous painters and their works of art, such as Picasso's *Guernica*, and explain the history behind them. We had to read a book on the life of Vincent van Gogh and view many of his paintings. Then we studied Renoir, Gauguin, and Rousseau, who painted the jungles and all the wild animals. Our teacher told us that Rousseau was so engrossed in his painting that the animals became alive in his mind, causing him to run out of his house and scream, "The tigers are after me!"

We also studied Degas' painted ballerinas, the famous Dutch painter Vermeer's interiors, and Rembrandt's *Belshazzar's Feast*. Now that I have studied the book of Daniel in the Bible, Rembrandt's painting holds more meaning for me, and a print of this painting hangs in my home today.

We visited Stockholm's museums and castles, which had been occupied by kings and queens for hundreds of years. We also found Sweden, a country rich with history, to be a beautiful country, mountainous and wooded with clear-flowing rivers. The winters were long and cold, and provided much skating and skiing. Since Sweden had remained neutral during the war, there were no ruins. Everything was neat and clean.

We were also required to attend the Royal Dramatic Theater, where we watched Henrik Ibsen's *The Wild Duck*. The main character's role was performed by Max von Sydow, a famous Hollywood actor, who also played the role of Jesus in *The Greatest Story Ever Told*.

The Royal Opera, yet another outlet of cultural learning, was a beautiful building across the river from the Royal Palace. Here I had the privilege of learning about world-famous composers and listening to their music.

During the summers many Swedish students traveled to France and England to learn more about those cultures and practice the languages they had been taught in school. I, too, was eager to learn, realizing how much education I had missed as a result of the war and my ill health. Now I had a chance to catch up.

Because the teachers and students were very nice to me, I never felt like an outsider. In fact, they found me interesting and asked me on several occasions to stand in front of the class and relate my war experiences. I was able to answer many of their questions and give them a broader view of the war, since their country was fortunate not to have experienced it.

By now Mother was working for a very nice family, the Lindmans, who lived within walking distance of our little rental. Mr. Lindman had been a delivery boy as a young man, but had good sense when it came to investing. As soon as the war was over in Germany, he began buying many shares in Volkswagen, which were cheap at that time. Of course, his father-in-law didn't think much of his business venture. "What are you going to do with all those shares, Olaf, paper the walls?" his father-in-law would tease. And all of Olaf's well-meaning friends laughed too—but not for long. Volkswagen became a very popular car, not only in Germany but worldwide. He sold some shares after the value went up, bought apartment buildings, and received a nice income from the renters. Thus he could afford a cleaning lady, my mother, to work for his wife.

The Lindmans had two children, Johan and Christina. Christina and I were close in age, so I wore her hand-me-downs, which were nice, quality clothes. Mrs. Lindman was a good and noble woman, and since they themselves came from humble beginnings, they treated me as an equal. When Christina had her friends over, they included me. When Christina enrolled in evening classes to learn typing, Mrs. Lindman enrolled me as well. I loved her, and to this day I appreciate all that she did for me.

Even after we left the country, Mrs. Lindman and I wrote letters and stayed in touch. She asked once what I would like as a memento of our friendship, and I replied, "A Swedish-English dictionary." She was very pleased and promptly sent one, which I still treasure.

Life continued for us uneventfully until one day we received a registered letter from the Swedish Red Cross. To our shock and surprise, enclosed was a letter from Babushka Natasha addressed to my father and mother. It was the first contact we had with her since that morning years ago when we said our goodbyes at the train station.

With trembling hands, Mother opened it and read:

Our Dear Son, Nikolai, Dusia, and Allachka,
Where are you and how are you all? We haven't heard from you in so many years. But we applied to the Swiss Red Cross through our government and hopefully this letter will find you alive and in good health. We miss you all and love you. Please come back home.
Your Mother and Father

Poor Mother almost fainted. Imagine the dread that filled her as she sat down to pen a reply, explaining everything that had happened to us during our 10 years of separation. Father had died in a concentration camp, she had remarried, we had to come to Sweden because of my tuberculosis, and she now had a baby boy with her new husband.

A few weeks later we received another letter from Babushka Natasha. We later discovered these letters had been written by my aunt Katya, who had returned home after the war. Babushka Natasha poured out her pain and suffering, but there was no accusatory tone in her letter. She knew Mother's character and that the things that happened in our lives were beyond her control. She was also sensible about the situation—a young widow should remarry. Mother was relieved that they were still friends and began buying warm clothes to send to them, knowing it was just one of many needs they had back home. It was winter, and in Sweden there were plenty of good, warm clothes to share.

Soon afterward, another letter arrived. This one was addressed to us directly from Mother's mother, Grandma Barbara. Mother was so happy! Grandma Barbara had remarried, and Mother's sister, Alexa, was alive and well. Grandma Barbara would outlive a third husband, dying at age 93. To Uncle Vanya's frustration, Mother now had two families to supply with warm clothes.

To our delight, however, they sent us whatever family photos they could spare—a real treasure, since all our pictures had been lost in the bombing of the camp. My aunt Alexa also sent updated pictures of herself and her mother and stepfather, which prompted my mother to write: "My dear Sister Alexa, why is it that in all of your pictures you always look so sad and you never smile? Also, at your age how is it you never married?" Those were hurtful questions and Mother should have known better, but the reply came: "Dear Sister Dusia, you ask me why I look sad. You know how hard our lives have always been. I did not get married because many of our men perished during the war, and many of those who did make it home were invalids. As you can see, there is not much to smile about." After reading the letter, Mother felt humbled.

We were grateful to be in touch with our families again, but things were not going so well in our family. Even little George didn't bring happiness and joy to Uncle Vanya, who was chronically depressed and locked his bedroom door when he left for work each day. In fact, he began to resent all the attention Mother and I paid to my little brother. If Mother brought home some cold cuts, he would write his name on the wrapping paper and not allow us to have any. They were his, and we knew that if we crossed him, he would become violent.

I especially remember one day when he called me into his room and wanted to talk to me. I was pleased that he took the time to have a conversation with me. I sat there with a broad smile on my face and waited, an 18-year-old girl full of hopes and dreams. "Well," said Uncle Vanya, "what are you planning to do with your future? What aspirations do you have?"

My heart leaped with joy. I was dying to share my thoughts and plans with him, so I poured out my heart to this man. But my words were met with a frown. "You know, Alla, your plans will never pan out."

"Why not?" I asked in disbelief.

"Because you don't have what it takes, and you will grow up to be an idiot."

Nevertheless, the strangest thing happened. At that moment I felt as though a divine presence encompassed me, as though God Himself was comforting me and letting me know how much I mattered to Him.

I looked at Uncle Vanya and continued smiling. This seemed to enrage him. "Get out of my sight!" he ordered in disgust, which I gladly did.

A number of friends who were now settled in America sent us care packages, Christmas gifts, and long letters describing how well they were doing along with pictures to prove it. They promised to help us find jobs and a place to stay if we would come. This was very tempting, of course, because we were not doing well financially. Even Lydia, Mother's dear friend and roommate from school, who was now in Belgium with her family, sewed and sent beautiful little outfits for George.

Finally, after spending almost five years in Sweden, Mother and Uncle Vanya decided to immigrate to America. I was close to 20 by then and able to take care of myself. To be honest, I was happy when I waved goodbye to them at the airport. At the time the only one I would really miss was George, who was 4 years old. I was accustomed to knitting little sweaters and sewing pajamas for him and taking him to day care by bus. Sometimes people thought I was his mother, but we just smiled at one another and kept our little secret.

One of my favorite memories of George is the day I forgot to put his mittens on when we went out. "Now, George, don't tell Mother I forgot your mittens." It was very cold, and Mother had already warned me not to forget. He nodded his head vigorously in agreement. The moment we arrived home that afternoon he marched straight to Mother and said, "Mama, I am *not* going to tell you Alla forgot to put mittens on my hands!" Mother couldn't resist a smile.

After my family left, I lived in a Salvation Army building while attending a business trade school. Once more I was learning typing, shorthand, and bookkeeping, and I was continuing to study Swedish and English.

There were several other young girls I made friends with who also stayed in the Salvation Army building, but attended different schools. I developed a wonderful friendship with a nice, quiet, intelligent girl, Birgit, with whom I still keep in touch today. We have so many wonderful memories, and it warms my heart each time she sends me letters and pictures of her family.

I found employment as a secretary and was on my own, so I rented a room in a very nice women-only apartment. I still continued to develop friendships, but now young men started to enter my life. I liked them and they liked me, but we could never develop a serious relationship. After all, I was not a "good catch": no family, no money, a limited education, a heavy Slavic accent, and not completely healthy, since I was still receiving pneumothorax treatments each month. The young men's families were afraid for their sons. After all, I was a former TB patient. But I didn't blame them; I would have felt the same.

In fact, once when a young civil engineer from my office took me out on a date, he stopped on the way at his parents' apartment, which was located across the street from a park. He asked me to sit on a park bench and wait while he had lunch with his parents. I was able to see them through their window as the young man and his father began a game of chess. As I sat on the bench, beginning to get cold, my affection for the young man cooled off as well. Later, after I left Sweden, he did call wanting to come and marry me and take me back to Sweden. I declined—I had no interest in sitting on a cold park bench. I later heard he married a doctor, and that after a few years and two children, they divorced.

Meanwhile, I continued to go to the American embassy in Stockholm every six months to be screened by their doctor. He would check my lungs, take X-rays to see how the healing process was coming along, and then shake his head: "You can't go to America yet." As I would walk through the park to the streetcar after each visit, I would look up to the sky and cry inside, "O God, how long until I can join my family and friends?" Each time I experienced keen disappointment.

Mother wrote letters and sent money and packages containing nice dresses. I could see they were doing well, and I was happy for them. Most of my girlfriends were married by now and had homes, children, and nice cars. Yet here I was, alone, a stranger in a foreign country. I began dreading my visits to the embassy and that "not yet" answer.

As I look back, I see that this was a good experience for me, a lesson in learning to fully trust in God and rely on Him completely. And in His mercy, He protected me from Uncle Vanya and his belligerence.

Although I had my moments of loneliness and sadness, I was not morose, and I kept myself busy. I took sewing and cooking classes in the evenings after work and met interesting people. With the permission of my apartment manager, I rented a piano, and I took piano lessons for two years.

I had been in Sweden for nine years by this time. When I was 24, the long-awaited day arrived in early May of 1960, when one of the secretaries from the American embassy telephoned me at home. By now all the employees there knew me and my situation. "Miss Alla," she began. "Are you sitting or standing right now?"

"Standing," I replied.

"Well, sit down."

I quickly seated myself on the nearest chair.

"You can buy yourself a ticket and join your family in America!"

My life had always been such a roller coaster, and now I was overwhelmed with joy. I lay on my bed, my hands clasped behind my head, and stared at the ceiling, trying to mentally digest the news. My long-awaited dream had finally become a reality.

By the end of June I boarded a Swedish ocean liner, the *Gripsholm*. I had never experienced such luxury—wonderful food, dances, entertainment, a swimming pool, movies, and games on deck. It was all very surreal. After five days at sea, though, I became bored and was anxious to see my family.

We entered New York Harbor on June 29, 1960. It was a beautiful evening, and we were greeted by the lady of the harbor—that beautiful symbol of freedom known as the Statue of Liberty—holding her flaming torch high. The skyscrapers were lit, and the cars—so many cars!—busily drove back and forth. It was a spectacular view, one I had never seen before, and I thought, *I wonder what the future holds for me in my new homeland.* But the next day, all the lights and glitter were gone, and I saw only gray buildings and littered streets, but still lots of cars.

The next morning after breakfast, while our documents were being processed, we were treated like long-lost friends by the customs agents, who met us with smiles and welcomed us to America. They knew we were immigrants seeking freedom and a better way of life.

As I crossed the gangplank, I was met by Mother, a smiling Uncle Vanya, and a not-so-little George. Mother and I hugged and kissed, tears of joy spilling onto one another, and Uncle Vanya seemed sincerely happy to see me as well. George was a handsome 8-year-old and tall for his age. I was struck with how much I had missed him. How happy I was to put my arms around him!

As we drove through the streets of New York City to their home, Uncle Vanya chattered while pointing out sights of interest, such as the Hudson River and the famous Brooklyn Bridge we were crossing.

Finally we arrived home, several blocks from Prospect Park and the Brooklyn Museum, which we would later frequent, to an eight-family apartment building owned by a Russian family, immigrants just like us.

Mother, resourceful as ever, lived rent-free in return for janitorial services. She swept the sidewalk, washed the stairs from top to bottom, and in the early mornings and late evenings would "feed" the coal stove to keep the building heated and the water hot, making sure the fire never went out. This job meant no vacations, yet Mother invited friends to their home and had lots of company.

In addition, she had a part-time job with Brooklyn Jewish Hospital, which was within walking distance from home. She worked in the circumcision room, which was also a place of celebration for the families of the baby boys. She decorated tables with fresh roses from her garden and served bagels with cream cheese and lox, coffee, and Manischewitz wine. It was always a happy occasion for the families, despite the price the baby boys had to pay!

Many of these families had suffered through the Holocaust, and both they and Mother found a common bond because she had lost her husband in Buchenwald. For her good service she was rewarded with generous tips. She saved every penny, as Uncle Vanya also did with his wages from working in a lighting factory. Their goal was to achieve the American dream and own a home of their own.

Meanwhile George attended a school that was also located not too far from home. He was a bright boy, a good student, and did well.

I slept on the living room sofa in their apartment and did not complain—the family was finally reunited.

Three weeks after my arrival we were pleasantly surprised by two couples who dropped by to see us, especially me, since they had known me as a little girl in Somme Kaserne, the displaced persons' camp in Augsburg. I had been a flower girl in the wedding of the daughter of one of the couples. Later, after they had come to America, they had sent care packages to me while I was still in the children's hospital in Kempten.

Their driver, the son of the other couple, was not happy about driving the seven miles to our place just to see some girl who came from Sweden.

I happened to be in the cellar sorting through my meager belongings when they arrived. I came up wearing drab cleaning clothes, my hair was in disarray, and I did not look at all presentable. Nevertheless, the one woman who knew me kept hugging and kissing me, smiling from ear to ear. She also gave me $10, with which I would later buy my first dress in America.

The mother of the young man, whom I did not remember from Germany, took an instant liking to me and invited us all for a Sunday dinner, to which we agreed.

Meanwhile, the young man, Wesley, silently shook my hand when introduced. I could see he was unimpressed with me. The feeling was mutual. *What a bore*, I thought to myself. *I would never marry a man like him.* I was convinced he had no social skills, since he hadn't asked me how my trip was, nor said a word to me. I was not used to such an attitude. He later told me he had been thinking that he had seen prettier girls than I.

The designated Sunday arrived, and I showed up at their house with my hair nicely done and wearing the new $10 dress. Seated next to Wesley, I had many questions that only he could answer. We had come from the same displaced persons camp, knew the same teachers, and had mutual friends, even though he was 7 years older than I. After a few drinks, he opened up and became personable and talkative and brought me up-to-date on the lives of friends I had lost touch with during my stay in Sweden.

After dinner it became stuffy inside the house, so Wesley invited me to go out and sit with him on the balcony. He had brought with him some photo albums and showed me pictures of my former teachers and friends. I longed to see these people again, and this proved to be no problem. On the next Sunday a picnic was planned at which many Ukrainians would gather for dances and entertainment. Wesley offered to pick me up and take me so that I could meet several of my friends. He and his family had already been in America for nine years, were well established, and he had a nice car.

The weather was pleasant as we drove to New Jersey, and I excitedly peered out the window at my first glimpses of American scenery. Upon our arrival I felt at home at last—the Ukrainian music, the language, and the culture were all so familiar. After 10 years of separation, it was exciting to meet friends I had known from Somme Kaserne. What a joyful reunion!

At the end of the day, as we drove back to Brooklyn, Wesley stopped at a couple of roadside fruit stands and treated me to watermelon, since he knew I had had none in Sweden. And since I had eaten a banana only once in my life, it was a delightful experience to be treated one of them.

Wesley was very attentive, and he delighted in my innocence and simple joy. It pleased him to try to make me happy. I soon realized he was a decent young man and very friendly. Meanwhile, he was impressed with my appreciation and happiness for his every little attention, and the fact that I never asked how much money he made. I wouldn't have dreamed of asking him anyway, because I would have to calculate the exchange rate into Swedish currency, and I had never been very good in math. I was simply looking for someone to appreciate me. He proved to be supportive and, unlike greedy Uncle Vanya, reminded me of my father.

In the meantime, Uncle Vanya was getting tired of having me around. I was still sleeping on their couch in their two-bedroom apartment, and I was there for several more weeks.

And then Wesley proposed.

We had been visiting my friend Ludmila and her family in New Jersey. While she was cleaning up the dishes, Wesley and I sat outside on the back steps of their house. Suddenly Wesley turned to me and said, "Marry me, Alla. I promise to be a good husband."

At first I was startled. Even though I was nearing the age of 25, marriage had not been in my plans. I wanted to go to school and continue secretarial training. But then I looked at him closely. He lowered his eyes, probably shocked at his boldness, since he was on the shy side. Emotions flooded my mind. He seemed so sincere, honest, almost childlike, and I believed his promise to be a good husband. *Well,* I reasoned, *doesn't every girl want a good husband?* Besides, by now we were both deeply in love. So I said, "Yes."

When I shared the stunning news with Mother, she was furious! "What's wrong with you?" she yelled. Her face turned red, and her brown eyes blazed with indignation. "You have just come to America, and now you plan to marry the first guy you meet? Why don't you look around? There are many other young men!"

I could see her point. She wanted me to meet a man who could offer financial security. After all, Wesley was just a truck driver in New York City. I could see in her eyes that her hopes for me were dashed, but my heart was set. Uncle Vanya, on the other hand, was very eager for me to marry. Two days before the wedding he yelled at my mother, "Let her get out of the house. I can't stand the sight of her! Because of her I sacrificed five years of my life living in Sweden." So there were two of us who were happy about the upcoming marriage. He wanted me to leave, and I wanted to go.

When Wesley told Mother of his intention to marry me, her response was "I hope you realize what you are marrying. She has no money; her health is poor. In fact, she might even get sick again." Wesley's response was "That is no problem."

There is a saying among our people: A husband loves a healthy wife, and a brother loves a wealthy sister. I was neither of those.

Clearly Mother tried to discourage him from marrying me, but we were determined to go through with our plans. With Wesley still standing there, Mother looked at me and said sternly, "Go ahead and marry him. But don't come crying to me when things go wrong." And I never did. In fact, years later she longed to hear details and complaints about our relationship, but I never shared anything with her. Wesley appreciated that I always kept our marital details private and sacred.

Meanwhile Wesley's parents were pleased with the arrangement and tried to calm my mother's fears. They assured her they would help us financially if need be, and that they liked me very much.

esley (English for *Wsewolod*) was born near Kiev, the capital of
Ukraine. His mother, Sofia, was next to the youngest of seven sisters.
Her father served in the Russo-Japanese War as a medic, even though he
was a veterinarian by profession. When the war ended and he returned
home, he was offered a job as plant manager of a sugar factory and made
a good living.

At first he expressed disappointment that he did not have a son, but
later, during the war and persecution, he admitted that he was happy with
his daughters because none had to go to war.

Their home was very comfortable, as they had servants, all kinds of
musical instruments, and much entertainment. The seven girls were taught
how to bake, cook, sew, preserve food, embroider, and milk the cows by
working side by side with their servants. Their parents prepared them well
for life ahead.

When the time came for Sofia to be given in marriage, her parents looked
for suitors and set their sights on another well-to-do family. This family had
a son, Jacob, who was a gentle soul, very polite and spiritual. Jacob was the
youngest of 15 children, nine of whom died at birth or in infancy. The family
had their own private cemetery. But five older sisters survived, and Jacob
was the beloved little brother and son. He was driven to school by private
carriage and studied accounting, French, German, Russian, and Ukrainian.

Jacob's family also happened to be looking for a nice family with
a daughter who would be a fit wife for him. The day arrived when they
were invited to Sofia's home, and then the test came: she had to prepare a
sumptuous dinner all by herself to feed her potential husband and in-laws.
It was important to make a good impression. She passed the test, and the
wedding arrangements were made. There was no courting, no falling in
love. People were very practical.

After a while Jacob and Sofia became comfortable with one another,
and both were devoted to their first son, Wesley. A second son died in
infancy, and Sofia mourned his death for years.

Life was not easy for Sofia and Jacob. Jacob was falsely accused of a crime, arrested, and put in prison. He was released after his innocence was proven, but after that he was branded. Every time Jacob was hired as a bookkeeper at some factory or office, he would later be fired when it was discovered he had served a short prison term. He was under constant suspicion, and the war didn't help things. They lacked many necessities and lived under military bombardment the same as my family had.

Then both their families lost their homes as a result of the ongoing war and were at the mercy of their children. Thank God for good children—they all helped one another.

Later, 14-year-old Wesley and his parents were taken to a forced labor camp in Vienna, the capital of Austria. During their stay there, a private company contracted with the German government and requested that the labor camp give them prisoners to clean the rubble from the buildings that had been bombarded. In effect Wesley and his parents were freed, but worked for a pittance and lived in an abandoned, blown-out building.

When they learned that the Allies were closing in on Germany, Wesley and his parents, like so many of us, wanted to get away and be with the Americans. His father and a friend went to the railroad station to buy tickets. They were stopped and arrested by the Germans and detained overnight, but were finally let go after being interrogated. By the time they picked up Wesley and his mother, however, the train they were supposed to board had already left. What a disappointment! They would have to wait several more hours for the next train, but were able to board it without further incident.

As the train made its way through the countryside, it was forced to come to a halt and the passengers had to walk to the next train station because the railroad track was blocked by the wreckage of the train they had missed earlier. It had been mangled by bombs, and there were many casualties. They thanked God they had missed that train.

They finally arrived in Augsburg at the same displaced persons' camp where we stayed. Wesley and I belonged to our respective Scout clubs and attended the same camp church and school, but I was a kid and he a young man, so we did not interact and do not remember one another. However, our parents were acquainted. We had known the same teachers and priests and had grown up in the same surroundings. Therefore, we relate to one another very well because of our similar backgrounds.

esley and I married on Sunday, November 20, 1960. It was a beautiful Greek Orthodox wedding, and approximately 200 mutual friends attended to wish us well. It was such a happy occasion for all involved—for me to see all my friends who were once so poor, ragged, and hungry, now well dressed and driving shiny new cars, owning homes, and living the American dream; and for them to see me, having been alone and sick so far away and for so long, safely and happily settled among them. Even Uncle Vanya was amicable as we smiled at one another.

We settled into my in-laws' two-family brick house, also located in Brooklyn. I liked them very much. Like their son, they were very giving and generous and bought us brand-new furniture. Excited to have us living in her home, my new mother-in-law delighted in buying me nice dresses, especially since my wardrobe was meager. She had also paid for my wedding dress, since my mother had planned to purchase one from the thrift store. My mother-in-law was shocked. "My daughter-in-law will *not* wear a used dress," was her final answer. And so I ended up wearing a gorgeous new wedding gown.

We continued socializing with friends and family and attending church, a love that Wesley and I shared. We would later join the choir, and found the singing melodious and filled with love and praise to God.

Meanwhile, after much scrimping and searching, Mother and Uncle Vanya found the house of their dreams—a brownstone on Saint Johns Place in Brooklyn. At that time it cost them $19,000. It was like a work of art inside—hardwood floors covered with heavy, Persian wool rugs, solid wood doors, ornately carved trim, tall ceilings, large windows, magnificent crystal chandeliers, impressive crown molding, marble fireplaces with carved mantels, and solid wood stairs and ornate banisters running up all four floors. There were three floors of living space and the old servants' quarters in the basement.

At that time Mother received a letter from her mother, Grandma Barbara: "My dear daughter," she wrote. "So you and Vanya are planning to buy a house? Do not worry, my dear, about the money. I have many chickens. I can always sell eggs and send you money for a down payment." Mother smiled.

Mother and Uncle Vanya rented out the top two apartments and kept the basement and first floor for themselves. There was also a backyard in which Mother had a small garden of mostly roses, which she always loved so much.

The brownstone was huge and empty, but there were always thrift stores. The only new items Mother purchased were lace curtains from Belgium to hang over those tall windows. As she walked from work, she often found items discarded on the curb: sofas, chairs, paintings, and china dishes. The sets were not complete, but who cared? It was better than eating from tin cans.

Once she found a bed frame. It was large, but the wooden plank supports were thin and brittle and the mattress was on the skinny side. However, it was free and would do for the time being.

They later bought a television set and loved it, as it helped Mother improve her English, which she was studying at Brooklyn Community College in the evenings after work. She progressed well and kept up with the news, since it was, of course, broadcast in English.

Uncle Vanya, on the other hand, did not understand, and Mother had to translate for him. His inability to catch on to the new language was a real sore spot with him. His pride was in the way, though, and he wouldn't admit that he needed help learning it. He refused to make the effort that Mother was making to learn English. Instead, he would put her down at any opportunity, especially in front of friends. It became so bad that Mother's friends would say, "Dusia, how can you allow your husband to treat you like this? After all, you are an intelligent woman. Why don't you divorce him?" Mother would reply, "Oh, don't pay attention to him. I am used to it." But the seed was sown, and it would grow.

A few months later the signs were all there—I was expecting. Now there was even more excitement in the Czerkasij household. My in-laws were thrilled about their first grandchild. Mother, however, was more concerned about my health.

I wore maternity dresses before it was necessary because I couldn't wait for the arrival of the baby. And the most important thing we had to do was buy a baby carriage. My in-laws, Wesley, and I drove to a store that had a nice selection. The grandma-to-be demanded the best and most expensive carriage that could be had. For her, nothing seemed good enough. "Lady," said the exasperated salesman, "this carriage is good enough for Rockefeller." And so we purchased a blue-and-white carriage with shiny chrome wheels.

That September our little boy, Victor, arrived. Unlike my mother's birthing experience when I was born, my delivery was easy and my joy knew no bounds. The happiness and excitement was shared by all. We brought Victor home from the hospital to discover a brand-new piano in our living room, a gift and token of appreciation from my in-laws.

Two years later we were gifted with Yaroslav (we call him Jerry), our second son. As soon as I laid him in the crib for the first time, Victor threw a ball at his face and was surprised that Jerry didn't throw it back. He had expected an instant playmate.

Jerry's arrival was cause for more joy and celebration, and this time my in-laws rewarded me with a mink stole.

One sunny day three weeks later, while returning from a walk with my boys, I was met by the neighbor who owned the bike shop next to our house. Obviously distraught and waving his arms in the air, he yelled to me, "They shot the president!" I will never forget that painful day we lost President Kennedy.

One day there was much excitement in the Czerkasij household. A friend of my father-in-law's, a classmate way back from the Ukraine, was expected to visit. By now he was a bishop in our Ukrainian Greek Orthodox

Church. He was known to have suffered persecution and imprisonment by the Communists for his religious beliefs but had somehow made it to the free world.

Now he was honoring us with a visit. My mother-in-law began cooking up a storm and setting the table, and I was instructed on how to greet the bishop. "You will cup your hands," my mother-in-law directed. "He will place his left hand into yours while you kiss it. With his right hand, he will make the sign of the cross above your head, and pronounce a blessing upon you." I understood it was a very serious and important occasion, since he was a man of God.

While we sat at the table and enjoyed the excellent meal and company, it dawned on me that I should have my firstborn blessed as well. I sneaked downstairs where Victor lay wide awake and picked him up to bring him upstairs. "Most Honorable Father," I began as I respectfully approached the bishop, "please bless my son, also." The bishop stood up while Victor looked at him and let out a piercing scream. And no wonder—he saw a tall man dressed in black with a long, thick bushy beard and a large cross hanging around his neck. I was mortified as I held a kicking and screaming Victor, his arms wrapped tightly about my neck. "*Vitya*," I pleaded, "close your eyes and no one will see you." The bishop waited patiently as Victor calmed down, but I could detect a smile under his mustache as he blessed my son. Years later Victor would grow up to receive a master's in theology, teach Bible classes, and preach for many congregations.

Three years later I asked Mother to watch the boys while I kept an appointment with the same doctor who had delivered them. Pity and compassion was written all over her face as she looked at me. "Poor, *Allachka*, my poor child," she said, shaking her head.

"But, Mama, I *want* this child. We want to have a little girl," I explained.

Mother's expression immediately changed. She stomped her foot in exasperation and spat, "You're stupid! But," she continued thoughtfully, "if it's a girl, I'll throw a big christening party in the church hall. But if it's another boy, you take care of the celebration."

A year later Mother kept her promise and threw a party. God blessed us with a beautiful little daughter, Natalie, named after my babushka Natasha, and our happiness was complete. By now Victor was 6 and Jerry was 4, and they delighted in their little sister. Once, in fact, after I left the house with the admonition for the boys to watch their baby sister, I stepped back into the house to grab something I had forgotten. Thinking I was an intruder, the boys were standing guard at the top of the stairs with butter knives clutched in their fists.

By now we were living on our own in Brooklyn, which was closer to Mother's brownstone, and even though we had three young children, we hardly missed a church service. We wanted to instill in our children a love for God and church. Sometimes they were still asleep when we carried them out to the car. Yet I began to feel a spiritual emptiness. As much as I loved singing in my church, I felt a tremendous need to have a greater knowledge of God and to find out more about who He really is. "Dear God," I would often pray, "please lead me to the kind of people who worship You 100 percent. I want to follow You either completely or not at all."

God answered right away. I came down with walking pneumonia, and my face and hands broke out in boils. I could not move or lie flat on my back, and I was incredibly weak. Wet and hungry, baby Natalie cried pitifully, but I couldn't even pick her up.

For the sake of my overall health, we decided it would be best to move out of New York City and into an area where the air quality was better. My father-in-law gave us a down payment to purchase an old Victorian two-family house in Peekskill, which is across the Hudson River not far from Military Academy at West Point.

The city of Peekskill is located in northern Westchester County and has lots of history and wonderful buildings dating back to the early years of our great nation. Our house had been built by a banker in the late 1800s. It was spacious and well constructed with wood floors, tall ceilings, and a large porch. Later the house had been divided into two main apartments, with small, additional basement and attic apartments. The five of us lived in the four-room apartment on the second floor. We collected a decent income from the renters, but lots of headaches came with them and their situations. Wesley and I had to grow up fast and learn a lot.

Meanwhile, Wesley continued working as a tractor-trailer driver in New York City and commuted every day. He left before dawn and returned in the evening each day, his long days filled with the hard work of carrying heavy loads on his back. The responsibility of raising the children and handling the renters fell to my shoulders.

There was no Greek Orthodox church in our area, and I missed being able to attend services. People from many denominations came knocking on our door and sharing their literature and beliefs. I was respectful and open-minded, since I admired their dedication and knowledge of the Bible—a knowledge I didn't have. They invited me to their churches, and I went. Their services were different from what we were used to, but I liked them. Wesley did not object to my attending these churches because he wanted me to be happy. The children and I attended the Christian Alliance Church for four years and sometimes visited a variety of others. My interest in God continued to increase as my children learned Bible verses and Christian songs, and enjoyed arts and crafts at Vacation Bible Schools. But I never made any close friends. When the services were over, we did not interact again until Sunday morning.

One day I received a long-awaited letter from an attorney I had hired before we moved from the city. There had been much talk among us immigrants with respect to reparation from the German government for people like me—someone who lost her father and health as a result of the war. So the first thing to do was retain an attorney. I found a charming, elderly gentleman who gladly took my case and made certain that I qualified and had the potential of receiving compensation for my losses.

Even though I possessed my father's death certificate as proof of loss, it was not enough. I had to contact my doctor in Germany and ask him to write a letter to my lawyer, describing what he remembered about the condition of my health, since he was the one who did my lung surgery and began the pneumothorax treatments. Procuring this letter was no problem, since we were already in touch by regular correspondence. Apparently other former patients kept in touch with him as well and he was able to keep me updated on how they were faring. When it came to my request for information, he was gracious and happy to oblige.

My lawyer was pleased—all the facts of my case were well supported. But he also warned me that it would take a long time to resolve the matter. And it did. In fact, it took so long that I forgot all about it until years later on that spring day in 1972.

I stood staring at the certified envelope in my hand. With trembling fingers, I opened it. Enclosed was a check for $8,217.34. The attorney had retained his fee and the bank's commission for the transfer of money. I was struck by how cheaply my father's life was priced, and my happiness at receiving the check immediately turned to deep sorrow.

Since we were in need of a new vehicle, the check was a blessing and allowed us to purchase a brand-new Ford Torino station wagon. By now the children were 12, 10, and 6, and Mother suggested we all take a trip upstate to visit a couple whom she knew from the Ukraine.

After hours of driving, we finally arrived at our destination. Uncle Timothy and Aunt Vera had a dairy farm with 70 cows and much land. They had both worked in a factory when they first arrived in America and saved every penny they made. Being children of farmers, they loved the land and wanted a piece of their own. It so happened that this farm was for sale. There were hardly any houses around, and this house was spacious. When a shopping center with a gas station offered them a good price for a piece of their land, they accepted gladly. There was still plenty of land for the cows and their use.

Uncle Timothy was a potbellied, robust man with a short neck, and his face was leathery and weather-beaten. He smiled a lot and seemed happy and good-natured. He and the children immediately took to one another, and he offered them rides on his tractor after supper.

Aunt Vera was strict and did not smile. In fact, I never saw her teeth. Her hair was pulled back in a tight bun, and her face was prematurely wrinkled from constant exposure to the sun. She was a no-nonsense woman and yelled at Uncle Timothy a lot. It wasn't anything serious, just their way of communicating. He just smiled in response and went about his business. But Aunt Vera was also generous and good-hearted.

We were all happy to be together, and Uncle Timothy and Aunt Vera enjoyed the break from the monotony of running the dairy farm. They spent much time reminiscing with Mother, since the three of them had grown up together in the same village, gone to the same village school, and knew one another's families very well.

We ate eggs fresh from the henhouse, and Aunt Vera made a nice stew from their newly slaughtered calf. We also had fresh vegetables from their garden.

Eighteen years earlier Aunt Vera had unexpectedly become pregnant. She had not been happy about it, since they had their hands full with the dairy farm and had a daughter in college at the time.

She told us a story of how, while pregnant, she climbed up the silo ladder to check how much fodder it contained. As she neared the top, she heard sirens howling and looked down to behold two police cars and a fire truck surrounding the silo, and men frantically waving and yelling at her to come down.

She slowly descended, heavy with child and not appreciating her work being interrupted. When she reached the ground, her fury exploded, and she yelled at the well-meaning men. The poor men did not realize she hailed from a country where women swept the city streets, dug ditches, and worked on railroad tracks.

"How did they know you were up there?" Mother asked.

"Well," replied Aunt Vera, "some fool was driving by and called the police. He probably thought I was trying to commit suicide." We still have a good laugh over that story.

Soon afterward they had a healthy baby boy and were very glad for his help on the farm as he grew up.

After supper our last evening there, Uncle Timothy gravely turned to Mother and with much emotion announced, "Dusia, you remember my family was very poor. There were five of us children and only three pairs of shoes between us. If three of us played out in the snow, the other two had to wait inside for their turn to wear the shoes. Food was scarce, especially during the winter. During those times your father would pull up in a horse-drawn wagon and unload a sack of potatoes and one of carrots, jars of pickled tomatoes and cucumbers, a few loaves of bread your mother baked, and other foods we lacked. In his memory I want to give you and Alla the calf I just slaughtered."

We all sat solemnly at the table wiping tears as the memories flooded back. There had been so much sadness in our lives, and yet so much goodness and joy as well.

The next day Uncle Timothy had the veal ready for us to take, all cut up, frozen, and professionally packaged.

The day after we returned home, I received a call from a deaconess at the Christian Alliance Church I had been attending: Could I please prepare a meal for one of the families at church? The wife was in the hospital and the husband was home with their three small children.

The veal in the freezer was made into a big, flavorful pot of stew. When the young mother came home and the family returned to church, they couldn't thank me enough for my culinary skills. And I thought to myself, *Grandpa Gregory would be so happy to know his kindness reached all the way to the shores of America.*

Not long afterward Mother and I also had the privilege of flying out of state to visit another couple who lived close to their children and grandchildren. We had gone through the war together, lived in the same forced-labor camp, and together experienced the liberation by the American Army.

The reunion was a happy one. They lived in a nice house, had an orchard and garden, and the lady of the house was an excellent cook. We all sat at the table recalling the details of the past and the horrible experiences we had gone through. I asked the host what kind of a man my father was. "Gentle and a dreamer," he replied.

After dessert was served, our host retreated to the corner of the dining room and just sat there quietly. I could see that her mind was far away, and she looked sad. We stayed there a few days and then were ready to fly back home. As Mother and I sat snugly next to one another on the plane, I asked her why Aunt Milla had acted so strangely. "Oh," said Mother, surprised, "you noticed that?" I nodded my head. "Well," she continued, "I asked her husband the same question, and he said that she became like that the day they killed Nero. Apparently they participated in that violent act, and it has been haunting her ever since."

I then understood why God delayed Mother and me so that we did not rush back to our camp after the Americans fed us. He protected me from witnessing any more violence at my young age than I already had. I am also reminded of what God says: "'I will take revenge; I will pay them back,' says the Lord" (Rom. 12:19, NLT). When we hurt others, we hurt ourselves.

One day Wesley decided to take the family for a ride to explore our new surroundings since we still considered ourselves newcomers to Peekskill. On a small, quiet side street stood a little white church surrounded by a beautiful green lawn. I read the sign: "Seventh-day Adventist Church." I had never heard of this denomination, and laughed to myself. *What strange names people come up with for churches!*

On a chilly fall evening sometime later, my doorbell rang. As I opened it, a pretty young girl stood there smiling shyly. Her cheeks were rosy, and her eyes shone brightly. She was clutching a round can in her hand and asking for donations for a worthy cause. I admired her for going out and spreading her beliefs, but it made me feel a little guilty and purposeless. Soon her young husband, John, joined her. He looked like a boy, but introduced himself as a pastor. Since they both were small in stature, they looked like children to me, and my motherly instincts were stirred. I invited them inside, gave them my phone number, and asked them to come back and visit me. I had never given my phone number to strangers before, but for some reason I trusted those two. Before they left, the young pastor offered to pray. It was short, but my heart was touched.

They did call me, and they showed up a few days later. Only this time Bonnie, the pastor's wife, brought a loaf of tasty homemade bread. I was impressed. As they sat on the sofa, I asked them the name of their church. "Seventh-day Adventist," they replied. The light went on in my brain, and I smiled broadly. "I will come and visit your church some Sunday," I said. No response. Finally Pastor John mustered up his courage. "We don't worship on Sundays." I became confused. "When do you worship?" I asked.

"We worship on Sabbaths."

"I thought you were Christians," I said, disappointed.

"But we are," they said.

"Listen," I said, as patiently as I could, "Jewish people go to church on Sabbath; Christian people go to church on Sunday. See?"

They didn't seem to agree with me. They just sat there quietly.

Oh well, I thought, *I'll keep in touch with them and straighten out those two someday.*

Meanwhile, my husband and I continued attending social gatherings with our friends from the city. New Year's Eve was special, and that's when I put on all my finery: a long gown, mink stole, and jewelry. We were all dressed up, as were our friends.

The orchestra played, we all danced, and drinks were served. As I sat at the table next to my handsome husband, I experienced a sudden pain in my chest, so strong I could hardly breathe. As I looked at Wesley, sitting there with a cigarette in one hand, a glass of hard alcohol in the other, and tipsy, I realized I didn't like the sight of him this way. Then I looked at my own hand clutching a glass of liquor and I was shocked. Partying like this was not unusual for us, but it had never bothered me until now.

I turned to him, choked up, and said, half crying, "Wesley, at this very moment I'd rather be sitting in a church listening to a good sermon." Half drunk himself, he looked at me surprised. "You're crazy. Have another drink."

Yes, I thought to myself, *I must be losing my mind. I want to get out of here. We don't belong here.*

Somehow we made it safely home, but the longing to sit in a church and listen to a good sermon persisted.

Pastor John began visiting regularly, and I began having Bible studies with him. Ever wanting to learn, I drank in every word from the Holy Word of God. I was so proud of myself when I memorized Jeremiah 29:13: "If you look for me wholeheartedly, you will find me" (NLT). That promise applied to me—I was seeking with every fiber of my being. Of course, Wesley also had some questions, but sometimes he just wanted to prove the pastor wrong. The answers came straight from the Bible, and my husband couldn't win, which made him angry with the young pastor.

Meanwhile, I continued to visit other churches and happened to mention once that I was having Bible studies with an Adventist pastor. This news stirred up some passion. Those sweet women became agitated and told me there was some woman in that church who did not know what she was writing about. I had no idea who "that woman" was. Surely, if she were misleading the people in the Adventist church, they should get rid of her. But she remained a mystery to me.

One pastor called me up and warned me that the Adventists were fanatical about keeping the Sabbath, but that we could worship on Tuesday as a holy day if we wanted—it just didn't matter. Now I was really getting confused. But I continued to attend Pastor John's church and did not find the people extreme. They were friendly, and I was impressed that young and old alike were very well versed in Scripture.

We had potlucks, as they were called, after church service at which I shared some of my cooking. I discovered vegetarianism and learned to prepare these foods at home, but Wesley wasn't happy about it. "Just give me my meat, mashed potatoes, and gravy," he would say. Dutifully I did, but still incorporated those healthy new dishes. Our children attended Vacation Bible School during the summers, and I became active in singing with the little ones and helping them memorize Bible verses.

We also began developing new friendships. We would spend the day together in worship, fellowship, singing, and sharing how God was working in our lives. The people were clean-living and happy, and had a tremendous sense of humor.

In addition, this church promoted higher education and a health message. Since I had always needed to take care of my health (by now I had developed lupus, an autoimmune disease), the health message really appealed to me as well.

The time came when I felt that my search for a closer walk with God was over. I had finally come home. I announced to my husband that I wanted to get baptized, and again he was disturbed. Usually I was free to do things my way as long as I was happy, but not this time. He became irritable, started sulking, and was unmoved by my attempt to please him by being a good Christian wife. Our children felt the strain between the two of us, and it reflected the unhappy family situation. I trusted God's leading during this spiritual warfare, and He continued to guide.

Meanwhile, I read a book called *The Desire of Ages*, written by "that woman," Ellen G. White. When I finished reading the chapter titled "Gethsemane," I broke down and cried because it showed me so vividly how Jesus suffered for me, and that my sins and the sins of everyone in the whole world crushed His poor, innocent heart. "Lord Jesus," I prayed, "You went through all that just for me? Then take me and use me. I want to dedicate my life to You."

After 10 months of Bible studies I made my stand for God and was baptized. It was a very happy moment for me. I understood that there was nothing good in me, so I came to the Lord to become a new person. The first few days I was exhilarated and couldn't stop smiling and sharing my newfound faith.

Even though I was happy with my new life as a Christian, I began to experience what seemed to be tremendous spiritual and emotional warfare. It was as though I was constantly being reminded of the evil in my character, and every sin in my life was being pointed out. I began doubting my conversion and became depressed, which I had never experienced before. I couldn't sleep and cried easily over small things.

I was tossing and turning one night, so I decided to sleep on the sofa in the living room because my husband needed rest. I was still awake and restless when suddenly the living room became pitch black. There was not a single ray of light, even though it was a corner room on the second floor and the street lights, along with the moon and stars, normally shone in through the windows. I sensed an evil presence and felt a heaviness pressing against my chest. I could hardly breathe and felt my heart pounding. Panic washed over me, and I began to pray, "O dear God, help me!"

Then, while the room was still very dark, I saw what appeared to be a fiery pen drawing the silhouette of a man standing at the end of the sofa where I lay motionless. I understood it to be the image of Jesus. But I was also made to understand that it was only a symbol of His presence in my life.

Suddenly the room was flooded with what seemed a heavenly light. I turned my head to look at the windows, but they and the walls were gone. Instead I saw angels descending from heaven in a long stream. They were not dressed in clothes as we know it. They appeared to be shrouded in a shimmering, light-blue mistiness that was in constant motion, as though a gentle breeze blew it. The borders of their sleeves and gowns were wide and embroidered with designs of gold. Their facial features were not clear, but it seemed they had long wavy hair. I sensed goodness and love emanating from them. The vision lasted only a few seconds, but it changed my life forever. Even though I would still continue to experience hardships through life, I never again doubted my conversion and complete acceptance by God.

Wesley finally began attending church with the children and me when we had guest speakers and would stay for the potluck lunches afterward. He admitted that he really enjoyed these occasions. The Holy Spirit was working on his heart, and he was responding.

Meanwhile, a group of members from this small Seventh-day Adventist church decided to open a vegetarian restaurant locally. The food was nutritious, delicious, and affordable; it was a rare treat for us to go out to eat because we still struggled financially. They also offered a stop-smoking class in the evenings. Wesley was a heavy smoker, so he attended the program. A film was shown depicting surgery on black, cancerous lungs—the result of smoking—and this impacted him greatly. They even had medical doctors presenting the facts, and Wesley, impressed by the professionals, soon chose to quit smoking.

But now the real test of faith came. At this point my father-in-law had already died of lung cancer, but Wesley's mother announced she would not set her foot in our house because of my change of religion. I knew she meant it, and for five years she didn't come visit us. We continued to bring the children to Queens to see her, even though our visits were tense to say the least.

Even though my newfound faith had been difficult for Wesley to accept, he mellowed little by little. Eighteen months later, in February of 1975, he and our oldest son, Victor, were baptized together. We continued to develop new friendships and attended a Christian camp that summer with wonderful programs for every age.

That fall Victor enrolled in Garden State Academy, a Seventh-day Adventist boarding high school in Tranquility, New Jersey. We had only $3,000 in a savings account, and we spent it all on his education. The students there not only studied but also worked. Some of the teachers were former missionaries, and all were fine, dedicated Christians. It was 75 miles away, and he came home once a month.

The next year, however, there was no money for Victor to return. The day came for school registration and Wesley had no intention of driving him back to the academy, so we notified the school that Victor would not be returning. Wesley, Victor, and I had a passionate argument. Victor packed his belongings and insisted on returning, saying, "God provided for one year; He will provide for the rest." I was torn between husband and son. Finally I said to both of them, "As for me and my house, I will serve the Lord." I retreated to my bedroom and knelt by the window, crying and pouring my heart out to God. While I was praying I heard the telephone ring. A moment later Victor walked in, smiling. The principal had called to inform us that one of the school staff had pledged a partial monthly payment toward Victor's tuition. The whole family knelt in a joyous prayer of thanks, and we promptly loaded the car and headed to New Jersey.

The year after that Jerry joined his brother at the same school. They both made many friends and enjoyed special programs.

Meanwhile, as we were enjoying our new lives, things were not going so well for Mother.

She came one weekend to visit and shared a terrible, albeit comical, story about herself and Uncle Vanya. One summer night, as they were sleeping in their Brooklyn brownstone, she awoke to a sound in the living room. She tiptoed down the hallway and pushed open the heavy sliding door while switching on the light. A short, skinny young man darted toward her with a knife in his hand. He just wanted to escape the house, but Mother acted quickly. She slammed the heavy door shut and held it tightly, trapping the intruder, while she yelled, "Vanya! Vanya! Help me!" Apparently he was in no hurry and did not come to her rescue.

Luckily, my brother George, by now a tall grown man, rushed up from the downstairs apartment where he slept. He held the intruder in a headlock while Mother called the police. Apparently the intruder had tried to cut the wires of the TV they had scrimped and saved to buy. Mother ended up giving him a bloody nose.

When the police arrived and saw what Mother had done to the would-be thief, they reprimanded her for taking the law into her own hands. She was furious and wanted to give them bloody noses too. While the police were handcuffing the culprit, out came Uncle Vanya.

"Vanya, why didn't you come when I called for help?" she demanded.

"What do you think I am, a fool?" he retorted.

"Well," she said to us, "apparently he didn't care too much whether I lived or died." And then I remembered the radio in Germany.

Meanwhile George finished his schooling as an X-ray technician and set his heart on moving to California. He got a job on a medical van and took off for San Francisco in pursuit of a new life and a bright future.

Life continued uneventfully for Mother and Uncle Vanya. They missed their son, but work kept them busy. For a while things were peaceful between the two of them—until the day it all came crashing down on their bed as well as their marriage.

Mother was sleeping soundly when she suddenly felt pain in her face. She jumped up, and there stood Uncle Vanya with one of his long-sleeved shirts in his hand. "Here, you lazy cow, sew the button that fell off," he ordered. While she was sleeping, he had swung the shirt at her with such force that one of the buttons on the sleeves whipped her face.

Obediently she sewed the button back on while Uncle Vanya went to sleep.

That was when Mother finally lost it. *I'm going to kill him, but how?* she wondered. Then she saw a large boom-box radio on the nightstand. She quietly unplugged it and positioned herself at the foot of the bed. *I'll crush his head*, she decided. As she lifted the radio high into the air and swung it with all her might, she lost her balance. The radio missed his head and knocked down the nightstand instead, and she fell on top of Uncle Vanya. The force of her fall caused the brittle boards supporting the mattress to crack, and the skimpy mattress folded in like a sandwich on the two battling spouses. How they struggled to get out of that predicament! After much pushing, pulling, and tugging, they finally freed themselves and burst out laughing. Shortly after this incident, however, Mother hired a divorce attorney. She loved him, but couldn't put up with his abuse any longer.

After 27 years of tumultuous marriage, Uncle Vanya was presented with divorce papers. He was shocked and literally suffered a stroke. He was sure he had Mother under his thumb, and never thought for a moment that she might leave him. Shuffling, slumped, mouth drooping, and speech slurred, he was not the same man after the stroke. He continued to try to come after her, but now Mother armed herself with a frying pan, which she skillfully wielded each time he tried to get too close to her. He would always look at her and say, "You could kill a person like that!"

"That's exactly what I intend to do!" she would reply.

The divorce ended up being bitter and painful for Mother, and she became depressed immediately afterward. She would call me and share her pain. I had only one answer for her: "Mama, pray."

They divided their brownstone in half, Uncle Vanya taking the basement and first floor, and Mother the third and fourth, the latter of which she rented out immediately. Because they were still under the same roof, however, the arguments continued, only more bitterly. It was after these arguments she would call me and cry.

I asked a Ukrainian Adventist pastor in the city to visit her regularly, give her Bible studies, pray with her, and give counsel. Later she told me, "If it were not for Pastor Roshak and his Bible, I don't how I would have ever made it." He proved to be a real blessing.

Now that Mother had financial independence, she began to enjoy her newfound freedoms, such as traveling to California to visit George, visiting

Alex and Lydia, who were settled in Connecticut by now, and visiting me frequently and spending time with her grandchildren. It was as though she came out of the darkness into light.

The time came, however, when they decided to sell their brownstone, and Mother moved to Peekskill to be close to us, while Uncle Vanya rented an apartment in the city. Mother bought a house on our street that had a large backyard, which she filled with flowers, especially roses. Strangers would walk by and see her working in her gardens. She always had a smile for them and would invite them into her "park" and give them tips on growing roses. In fact, she was featured in the local newspaper. Her house was two blocks from the city hall, and she became friends with then-mayor George Pataki, who would later become the governor of the state of New York. His father had owned a roadside fruit stand by their family orchard, and young George learned early to help on the family farm, especially in picking the berries. The Pataki family had immigrated to America many years previously, and we used to buy our produce from them and had nice chats together, since we also came from Europe.

So Mother would pick beautiful bouquets and bring them to city hall. She knew the inspectors, the secretaries, and the deputy mayor, Mr. Jackson. Of course, it also gave her opportunities to tell those dear people how to run the city! Sometimes she came up with good suggestions, many times not, but the city employees appreciated her and her flowers and were very friendly.

Later came the day when she finally received her American citizenship. She loved this country and its people and was grateful for its freedom, beauty, and wealth. To really celebrate the occasion, she threw a party in her backyard. It was a beautiful summer day, her garden was exploding with color, and many friends came from the tristate area. Of course, Mayor Pataki and Deputy Mayor Jackson attended as well. Since only a few of the people knew Mayor Pataki, I had the privilege of introducing him to our friends. He was a very nice gentleman, tall and handsome, and we were impressed that he took the time to visit with us.

When Mother wasn't avidly gardening, she continued her hobby of being a businesswoman by turning her 11-room home into a boardinghouse. Because it was located just a few miles from Indian Point, a nuclear power plant located on the Hudson River, many of the temporary engineers stayed in her home during the workweek.

She also found another hobby when she discovered a little produce market. There was a dumpster behind the store where, on Saturday afternoons, the owner threw out large quantities of older produce. That piqued Mother's interest. She would take her laundry cart, which was lined with a plastic trash bag, and "dive" into the dumpster. I understood why. Coming from such a poor background and hating waste, she was compelled to "rescue" the potatoes, onions, carrots, beets, and celery from being thrown away. Besides, she probably thought of it as her personal root cellar and felt very comfortable with that bin.

One day, as the upper half of her body was inside the bin, her legs dangling outside above the ground, she heard someone blowing a car horn. She was very engrossed in her project and did not appreciate being so rudely interrupted. As she steadied her feet on the ground, she saw a white Cadillac stopped just a few feet away from her. There at the wheel sat a nicely dressed gentleman, smiling broadly and waving dollar bills in his hand. "Hey!" he called. "Come here, I'll give you a few dollars." After realizing that he mistook her for a vagrant, it was her turn to smile. She sauntered up to the car and said to the man, "Listen, honey, you put your money back into your wallet. I don't need it! Do you know how much I have in the bank?" Looking triumphantly at me as she relayed the story, she laughed. "I told him, but I won't tell you! But that man's smile disappeared, and he took off in a hurry!"

Because of Mother's thrifty ways and her resourcefulness, she was very philanthropic and able to support a number of charities and orphanages, and even helped with my children's tuition bills when most needed.

In the spring of 1979 the day came for Victor to graduate from high school. Since he had always been my mother-in-law's favorite grandchild, I invited her to his graduation. I could see that she struggled with her decision because she had not visited us for so long, but in the end she chose to attend. We picked her up in the city and drove to the school campus, where we all stayed for the weekend program.

And then the miracle happened—Wesley's mother had a change of heart. She looked at the students around her and was impressed by how nice these young people were. She enjoyed the music, singing, and beautiful surroundings. She kept nudging me, saying, "Look how happy these people are! Look how they smile!" Her attitude began to soften.

Afterward, she visited the Ukrainian Adventist church in the city and made new friends. I obtained a Ukrainian Bible, which she began reading for herself. Many times she would look at me and quietly say, "Alla, I didn't know. I just didn't know. People told me so many negative things about your beliefs, and now I see how untrue they were."

Our second son, Jerry, graduated two years later, and both brothers attended Southern Missionary College in the Chattanooga, Tennessee, area while their sister, Natalie, enrolled in Garden State Academy.

I began bringing in a small income of my own by cleaning homes and offices. Even though our three children worked at the schools, we really needed the extra income to pay the private school tuition. But my real love was being active in my church and helping with the children's programs. I felt as if I finally had found my niche in life.

We visited our sons in Tennessee every so often while they were studying and loved the surrounding area. By now Victor was seriously dating his high school sweetheart, Rene, a pretty, blond girl and daughter of a pastor.

Then came the year our lives caved in. My husband came home one day, dejected and shoulders drooping. The trucking company he worked for had shut down, and he was out of a job. In addition, our medical coverage was terminated. He applied for unemployment and looked for other truck-driving positions. There were a few positions available closer to home, but they offered less pay and required working on Saturdays. That was not an option for us, so I prayed continuously. We were aware that our faith in God was being tested, so we continued to trust in Him.

Finally he saw an advertisement in the local newspaper. Indian Point, the nuclear plant near our home, needed security guards. My husband applied, and to his delight, was accepted. Of course, he made sure to explain that he wouldn't work on Saturdays. It didn't seem to be a problem, so he attended several weeks of training and instruction required for the position.

Now, Wesley was a perfect candidate for this job. He had had two years of training in the U.S. Army and nine years in the reserves, and knew how to stand guard and handle a gun. Finally the training was complete, he passed the exam, and he was given a uniform. He looked so handsome in it; those shiny buttons made him look like a soldier again. He had always loved being part of the military.

Then the telephone rang one Friday evening, and a man on the line told him to put his uniform on and come to work for the night shift. Poor Wesley, he had to make a fast and difficult decision—and he did. "Sorry, but I will not work during Sabbath hours," he replied.

"OK," said the man, very much annoyed. "Then bring back your uniform first thing Monday morning." There went his work opportunity.

My mother's anger knew no bounds when she heard the news, and she shared her disgust with her friends. To her, our so-called faith was nothing but sheer stubbornness and stupidity.

One day as I was kneeling and scrubbing someone's bathtub (an easy position to pray in, by the way), I poured out my heart to God. Both Wesley and I were confused and torn between our obedience to Him, as we understood it, and the daily problems we were facing. And then it was as though I heard a voice in my head saying, "Ask Wesley to join you in cleaning houses."

I started calculating. If we cleaned three or four houses a day, five days a week, we would make much more than he would have as a security guard and would also be able to keep the Sabbath. I almost laughed out loud at such a brilliant idea. When I got home, I shared the plan with Wesley right away. He was not happy with the idea, since it was a blow to his male ego—from truck driving in New York City to cleaning houses with me. It felt so demeaning to him.

"Well," I asked, "why don't you at least give it a try?" With much hesitation and desperation on Wesley's part, our 12-year cleaning career began, and in all honesty we enjoyed it. Our clients called us "domestic engineers"!

But soon afterward my health began to fail. I became weak and anemic, couldn't keep up with my work, and had to see the doctor. He suggested surgery, and I was hospitalized for five days. Since we had no health coverage, the doctor allowed us to pay in installments, which took several years to pay off.

It took me a while to regain my strength, but our financial situation became so precarious we finally applied for food stamps to get us over the hump. We found out what it felt like to sit in Social Services, waiting and hoping to be approved. It was very humbling, and both our mothers were horrified that we would do such a thing simply because keeping the Sabbath was more important to us.

I was still recovering from surgery when we all traveled to Tennessee to attend Victor and Rene's wedding. Victor still had another year to go to complete his degree, but Rene had just graduated with hers. It was May of 1982, and the wedding was beautiful. The bride was petite and looked like a china doll; the groom was tall, handsome, blue-eyed, and rosy-cheeked from the excitement. They were so young then, but have found themselves happy to this day.

My brother, George, and his wife flew in for the wedding, bringing along their newborn son. We instantly fell in love with little Nicholas and ended up having a wonderful family reunion that weekend.

Sometime later I was able to resume work with Wesley. We established a creed for ourselves based on the apostle Paul's admonition: Servants, work as unto the Lord. We worked hard, were honest and dependable, and even became friends with the homeowners. God blessed us, and we began to slowly pay our debts, continuing to faithfully pay tithe and offerings, and always keeping our credit intact.

But the year wasn't over. Natalie had just come home for Thanksgiving break when we received a call from Victor in Tennessee: "Mom, everything is fine, but Jerry is in the hospital. There was an accident at the factory, and Jerry broke his arm." I thought he was joking, so Victor's wife, Rene, got on the phone and confirmed it was true. But we would soon find out it was more serious than just a broken arm.

Both boys had been working for a snack-foods manufacturing factory near the college they were attending. That evening Jerry had been alone in a room when the rollers of a large machine caught the sleeve of his jacket and pulled him in. As he was screaming for help, another worker came in to shut down the machine, just in time to save Jerry's life. The machine ground to a halt with Jerry's face against the roller. He had been pulled in up to his shoulder and sustained a crushed humerus, a severed radial nerve, multiple severed tendons in his wrist, and a severely bruised side.

The factory treated us kindly and immediately flew me down to be with Jerry. After three surgeries, physical therapy, and much trauma, pain, and suffering, his arm was partially restored.

Life continued uneventfully until 1986, when Wesley's mother died at the age of 79. Her loss was easier to bear, since by then our relationship had been restored. A few years later Uncle Vanya died of Alzheimer's. At that time he was in a nursing home facility in California near George. When George flew Vanya's remains back to be buried in New Jersey, George's luggage was sent to Canada. "Good thing Vanya was not sent to Canada," Mother commented.

Before Uncle Vanya died, however, Mother and I had the opportunity to visit him one last time. As we entered his room, his face lit up with joy upon seeing George. "Nicky!" he exclaimed. "Oh, Nicky," he kept repeating earnestly. "You know, I keep getting letters from Mother and Father."

Nicky was Uncle Vanya's brother, and we knew his parents were not living, because they would have been more than 100 years old.

Then the nurse walked in and George introduced her to us. She smiled and showed us her hand. Uncle Vanya had broken one of her fingers, and it hadn't healed properly. "That rascal," she said, smiling, "locked me in here and grabbed my hand, twisting it so that my finger broke." We felt sorry for the nurse, but were not surprised. Mother fared worse than that during their marriage.

During the visit Uncle Vanya appeared content, but then his face became serious.

"Vanya," Mother asked, pointing at me, "who is that?"

His gaze softened as he looked at me. "She's a nun!" He almost smiled and seemed pleased with himself that he knew the "correct" answer.

"And who do you think I am?" continued Mother.

"The devil knows!" he snapped.

Later, after we buried Uncle Vanya and were leaving his graveside,

I heard Mother say somberly, "What a pity, Vanya. We could have lived happily together." I detected sadness in her voice.

But then she began pulling the red and white carnations out of the funeral wreath that lay by the grave. She looked like a mischievous little girl who was taking something that did not belong to her. Beaming in reply to our questioning looks, she laughed, "He doesn't need them now. I'll enjoy them more than he will!"

When *perestroika* (reconstruction) occurred during President Reagan's administration and the borders of the former Soviet Union were opened to the West, we invited my aunt Katya, my father's sister, to come visit in the early 1990s. Mother paid for her trip, and after getting the visa cleared, Aunt Katya arrived at Kennedy Airport. What a happy reunion! The last time she had seen me was 52 years earlier, when I was 6 years old. She stayed with us for nine months. We took her sightseeing and toured New York. She was especially impressed with our shopping centers and supermarkets. She would stand in the produce aisle in complete awe, amazed by the sight of all the fruits and vegetables; we bought anything she requested. She also asked when the produce would be removed, thinking it was just a show promoting American propaganda.

One day I said, "Aunt Katya, since I can't do anything for my father, I will do it for you, his sister." She appreciated that, so we had her eyes checked and bought her new eyeglasses, took her to the dentist, and took her to the doctor to have her heart checked. She was in good health. When she went back home, she took many things with her, including money generously given to her by our Ukrainian friends.

We had lots of time to catch up on all the happenings of the 52 years we had been separated, but I mostly wanted to know about Babushka Natasha. My poor babushka suffered the loss of her youngest son in the Russo-Finnish war. Then came the letter from Sweden when Mother wrote that my father died in Buchenwald concentration camp and that she had remarried. Later another uncle of mine died of cancer, Grandpa Anton died shortly thereafter, and Babushka Natasha's poor heart couldn't bear all the loss and sorrow, and she died too. Aunt Katya had kept Babushka Natasha's gold wedding band, brought it to America, and gave it to my daughter, Natalie. Aunt Katya was very pleased that we had named our baby girl after Babushka Natasha.

I also asked Aunt Katya why no one spoke of God when I was a child, except to threaten us kids with punishment by Him. Didn't they believe in Him?

"Yes, we did," she said, "but we did not talk about Him because if somebody reported us to the authorities, we would be punished for it. We did believe in Him, prayed secretly, trusted Him, and hid Him in our hearts."

I understood what she was saying because I do remember that even though no one talked about their beliefs, people lived them. Poor as we all were, we helped one another, shared our meager supplies, and looked out for one another's welfare.

I asked, "What kind of child was I?" Her answer was "Not a pleasant one. We were all grown up, and we spoiled you. You were always getting into trouble. And your head was full of sores because of the poor sanitary conditions. We shaved off your hair regularly to keep lice from dwelling there, so you weren't a pretty sight either." Our people are very frank by nature, to say the least! But this was all true. We had no soap, nor running water. All of us kids had our heads shaved, especially during the summer months; but as I think back, we were a happy bunch. We invented our own games, and the Torets River was close by, where we could splash to our hearts' delight.

During the time Aunt Katya was staying with us, Natalie and I flew to St. Petersburg, Russia, to meet Katya's daughter and her husband. We spent two wonderful weeks visiting the Hermitage, which included famous palaces, museums, and *sobors* (cathedrals). We also visited the Czars' Village. Every day from morning to evening my cousin, an engineer, and her husband, a retiree from the Soviet military, took us all over the city. The collection of the Hermitage contained many paintings from the Bible, and I was able to tell them the stories behind the paintings. Having just come out of Communism, they had very little knowledge of the Bible.

I asked my cousin to tell me more about our babushka Natasha, and she shared with me a humorous incident. The very first time Babushka Natasha watched a television set, her eyes grew wide with wonder. She viewed a sports arena with thousands of men in attendance. "Imagine," she remarked in awe, "how many yards of material were needed to sew pants for all those men."

Chapter **36**

ventually the time came for us to retire. Our years were catching up with
us, so we moved to the Chattanooga, Tennessee, area at the invitation of
our oldest son, Victor. By now he was settled there with his wife and their
two young sons, Alex and Nikolaus, so we decided it was time to be near
family and enjoy our grandchildren. We sold our house in Peekskill, New
York, and moved south to enjoy the climate, community, and wonderful
new friends.

A few years later our son Jerry decided to join us and settled nearby.
Presently he is a respiratory therapist and is married to Stefanie, a beautiful
nurse he met at the hospital where they both work, and blessed with
Conner and Emily, their precious children.

More recently our daughter, Natalie, settled here as well, along with
her husband, Jim, who is like another son to us, and their lovely daughter,
Shelby. They keep busy with their own engineering practice. We feel truly
blessed and content to be surrounded by all our children and grandchildren.

Mother, however, wanted to maintain her independence and stay in
Peekskill, New York, where she had her home, social life, and garden. But
time was catching up with her as well, so in November of 2001 she sold her
home and moved into a retirement apartment two blocks away, across the
street from city hall. One month later, on the eve of my birthday, I received
word that Mother died in her sleep at the age of 84, 57 years after my father
was taken away on the day of my eighth birthday.

Over time, as I shared my life experiences with friends at church
here in Tennessee, people began asking me to share my story with local
churches, clubs, public and private schools, and the university. I was even
interviewed on local radio and in newspapers, especially during Holocaust
Week, since I have so much experience that relates.

It gives me great joy to share how wonderfully God has led in my life
and watched over us. Despite the pain and losses we experienced, we always
felt God's presence, and this gave Mother, me, and many other survivors
the courage and strength to bear it all.

What also gave me the will to survive and to have a positive outlook on life was the deep love of my babushka Natasha and my father, Nikolai. There was no need for words—I was simply loved, much as our Father in heaven loves us.

Mother and I were very different from one another, but I respected her greatly, as she was a very honorable woman. Although she herself was starving, she gave her ration cards to my father to save his family, which was the height of unselfishness. That was her way of showing love. While our camp was burning and we were running, her grasp on my hand is one thing I vividly remember. She wouldn't let go of me and made sure she pulled me to safety. Sometimes I wonder whose hand it really was.

Even Uncle Vanya had redeeming qualities. As I look back, I realize that life was not kind to him, either. He never spoke of his first wife or their daughter, who must have been close to my age, or of his loss. I'm sure he missed them and experienced some pain when he married another woman with a child not his own.

I find there is a reason for everything that happens in life. So far I have received hundreds of letters from students with whom I've had the privilege of sharing my experiences. If only adults realized what jewels there are among those young people. They open their hearts to me in appreciation for speaking to them, and I learn much from them as well. My message to them is always the same: Respect your parents and teachers, because they are the people who love and care for you the most. Get a good education, but above all, make God the center of your lives.

I do not know how much time I have left on this earth to continue sharing the love of God. But I have seen Him working and leading in my life as well as in the lives of others. And if I had to live my life over again, I would gladly do so just to be able to share with everyone the knowledge of what a great God we serve.

My search is over, and I find that I have come full circle. In my heart I have joined, and become a part of, that precious circle of praying prisoners in the bomb shelter during that night so long ago. My hope and prayer, dear reader, is that you too find deliverance in our mighty Lord!

This is my story, this is my song, praising my Savior all the day long.

Another Powerful Testimony

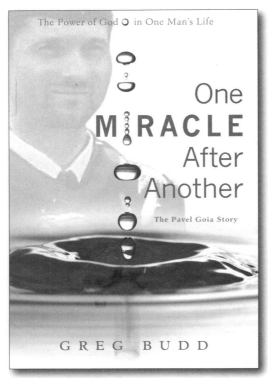

The Power of God ○ in One Man's Life

One
M I RACLE
After
Another

The Pavel Goia Story

GREG BUDD

One Miracle After Another
Greg Budd

Pavel Goia knew when he was 5 years old that God had called him to speak for Him. Yet by the time Pavel reached his teens, having a good time with friends was far more important to him than his family's religion. And communist Romania wasn't exactly friendly to Christians.

But God got his attention one fateful night, and his life took that proverbial U-turn. Pavel made a covenant with God, and his dedication to that covenant was tested almost immediately. But he stayed true, and miracle after miracle followed in behalf of this one young man who trusted every aspect of his life completely to God.

The results of his unwavering loyalty to God? Four thousand pounds of glass suspended midair in a bottomless crate, a law passed by President Ceauşescu that forced a university to allow Pavel to continue his education, a large shipment of Bibles smuggled by unsuspecting police, and a dead boy raised to life—just to name a few.

Oh, yes, miracles still happen—one right after another. 978-08280-2496-9

Availability subject to change.